Penguin Nature Guides

Birds

of Sea and Coast

Lars Jonsson

Translated from the Swedish by Roger Tanner
Edited by Jim Flegg

Penguin Books

Penguin Books Ltd, Harmondsworth,
Middlesex, England
Penguin Books, 625 Madison Avenue,
New York, New York 10022, U.S.A.
Penguin Books Australia Ltd, Ringwood,
Victoria, Australia
Penguin Books Canada Ltd, 2801 John Street,
Markham, Ontario, Canada L3R 1B4
Penguin Books (N.Z.) Ltd, 182–190 Wairau Road,
Auckland 10, New Zealand

Fåglar i naturen: Hav och kust first published by
Wahlström & Widstrand 1977
This translation published 1978

Printed in Portugal by Gris Impressores, Cacém
Filmset in Monophoto Times by
Northumberland Press Ltd,
Gateshead, Tyne and Wear

Contents

Preface

When planning and arranging a field guide the most useful and interesting information must be chosen from the wealth available. The plates must illustrate as many plumages and variations as possible, but at the same time be large enough to bring out the finer details in plumage patterns; this is not an easy balance to strike. The task has been made easier by dividing the European species between five volumes. There are other advantages in this arrangement which in my opinion outweigh any disadvantages. My aim has been to use the limited printed space to bring out what is not already evident from the illustrations. I trust that the reader will be able to link the two.

I would like to extend a special word of acknowledgement to Stellan Hedgren for his close co-operation. My thanks are also due to Gunnar Brusewitz, Håkan Delin, Wolf Jenning and Lars Svensson for their views and comments, and to Lars Fält who helped to write the introduction.

L.J.

Introduction

This is the second volume in a series of five which are planned to cover all bird species regularly found or nesting in Europe. It deals with those species which for some period of the year have as their principal habitat the open sea or coastal areas. The area covered is the continent of Europe, excluding the Mediterranean area and the Iberian peninsula.

Of course, there is no hard and fast biological boundary between lakes and sea or between the seashore and its hinterland. Most land birds may be observed in coastal areas during migration, during winter or in the nesting season, but the great majority are not connected with the biology of the seashore and are therefore omitted here.

The Baltic, with its brackish water, occupies an intermediate position between freshwater areas and sea, as do many estuaries and enclosed bays. Some of the birds omitted from this volume, such as grebes, swimming duck, certain diving duck (*Aythya*), coot and snipe, occur regularly by sea in these and similar biotopes. Moreover, species such as Montagu's harrier, hen harrier, merlin, kestrel, short-eared owl and several small birds (see p. 117) also inhabit fields of various kinds close to the sea. But the seashore is not their real, principal habitat, hence their exclusion. Species nesting inland (mainly on mountain and tundra) but migrating and wintering along the coast have been included, on the other hand, as they spend much of the year at sea or on the coast, and are most likely to be seen there. There are some omissions such as the great crested grebe, red-necked grebe, pintail and wigeon; these could be classified as birds of the seashore, but have not been included as they are better dealt with in other volumes. By doing this, the practical difficulties of field identification can be eased, and advantage taken of similar species and groups being placed in the same volume. Finally, Europe is visited on rare occasions by stray individuals of species belonging to other continents. A number of American wader species are the most regular visitors of this kind, and therefore a selection is given.

Purple Sandpipers in winter plumage

Birds in their environment

Anybody who takes the time to really *watch* birds on a seashore will soon notice how different species prefer to keep to different types of coast and to certain parts of any particular beach. Barnacle geese will graze in the fields near the seashore; the shelduck keeps to the shallows, filtering small creatures out of the surface water and mud; the female eider dives (or 'ducks') after molluscs and crustaceans near the edge of the seaweed; other sea ducks dive for fish a little further out to sea and guillemots dive still further out, in deeper water.

The different sections of the environment (or biotopes) existing by the sea offer an enormous variety of foods, and substrates ranging from mud and sand to pebbles and rocks, each with its own vegetation. The various species have evolved in response to these conditions. They vary a great deal, of course, in the extent to which they specialize in particular types of food or habitat, etc. Many gulls are highly adaptable, which enables them to utilize a variety of foods, while the wader species are limited in this respect by their different beak shapes and leg lengths (p. 9). Food apart, the availability of suitable nesting sites and the occurrence of predators are also important items in the complex of factors governing coastal birdlife. In other words, these bird populations are regulated, in terms both of the number of individuals and the variety of species, by a number of different factors which combine to establish a balance between the population and its surroundings. The geographical range of a species, its commonness, the behaviour of individuals and other facets of its biology will all be seen in a more logical light if nature is regarded as a whole with all its constituent parts influencing one another.

Geology

The continent of Europe has a very complicated coast, featuring large inland seas such as the Baltic and the Mediterranean, large peninsulas such as Scandinavia and Italy, and large islands such as Britain and Ireland. The coastline is indented and broken by a multitude of bays and fjords, while in some areas there are extensive archipelagos. All this gives Europe the longest coastline of any continent in relation to its size. The coastal landscape has been, and is still being shaped by a host of different factors, such as the effects of the Ice Age, uplift, subsidence, erosion by waves and silting up in slow currents.

Besides the open sea, coasts are made up of an enormous variety of seashore environments, with an abundance of plant and animal life. Tidal

8

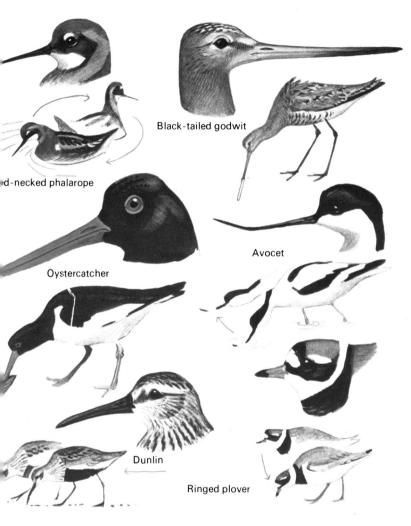

Beak shapes and feeding behaviours of some wader species: Phalaropes spin around on the water to make miniature whirlpools and then quickly peck at the small creatures and plankton stirred up.

The black-tailed godwit's long beak probes deep into loose soil (in summer) or mud for its prey. The oystercatcher prizes open mussels and other shellfish with its stout beak. Avocets skim small creatures off the surface water in rhythmic sideways sweeps. When the dunlin searches for food on the breeding grounds it walks, head down, pecking at the ground surface; in winter on the coast it usually probes into mud like the black-tailed godwit. Lapwings and most of the plovers stand still, watching or listening for their prey, and run to seize it before resuming their upright stance. Watch for other types of feeding behaviour displayed, for example, by the turnstone and sandpipers of the Tringa family.

beaches, cliffs, sandy beaches washed by the sea, sand dunes and saltmarshes are all different and all make their specific demands on the organisms which in turn constitute the foundations of coastal bird life.

Climate

Europe is a temperate region customarily divided into three climate zones: continental, maritime and Mediterranean. Their boundaries are indistinct, particularly between the first two. The maritime climate, which mainly affects western Europe, is characterized by a relatively slight difference in temperature between winter and summer and between night and day. The reason why west winds are so common in northwestern Europe is that most areas of low pressure pass on a line to the north of Scotland and Norway; the winds to the south of a low are always west winds. These come from a sea which is warm in relation to its latitude and whose warmth is partly due to the winds themselves bringing warm surface water from the Gulf Stream to the coasts of western Europe. These west winds make for mild winters in the northwest. The barrier effect of the Scandinavian mountain range makes winters drastically colder further east. Large areas of the Baltic and the Gulf of Bothnia (as well as the lakes inland) are covered by solid ice in winter. This explains the northeast-to-southwest migration of most water birds in northeastern Europe and Asia.

Life on the seashore

We have seen how the different bird species are dependent for food on particular groups of plants and animals, which in turn are adapted to particular types of seashore. As sources of food, sea cliffs and sand or mud beaches are the most fruitful. Cliffs are fairly stable and the animals there are often stationary, such as sponges, sea anemones, barnacles, mussels and limpets. Cliffs often have an abundant flora of seaweed which supports and protects a large number of organisms such as crustaceans, molluscs and fish.

The relatively stable shores of fine sand or clay are inhabited by many excavating species, mainly worms and molluscs, but also by many crustaceans and sea-urchins (see also *Tidal beaches in western Europe*, below). Boulder shores are virtually biological deserts, and few birds inhabit them.

The chemical and physiological composition of the seawater determines the distribution of species to a great extent. Many, for example, are sensitive to changes in the salt content of the water, so that the Baltic, with its brackish water, has a completely different fauna from the North Sea. For the same reason there are many species normally associated with lakes which occur as residents in the Baltic, such as the velvet scoter, goosander, common sandpiper and Caspian tern. Estuaries, particularly tidal ones, demand a great adaptability and are sometimes inhabited by fewer species, although each of the species occurring may be very numerous (see below). The rising tide may increase the salt content of the water some distance up the estuary from, say 1–25% twice daily.

Birds not only eat plants and animals along the seashore but also live on insects, spiders and other invertebrates. Some live on seaweed, some on dead organic material accumulating on the seashore and others will be found devouring dead animals washed up by the sea. Many species also live on fish, small creatures and plankton, as well as fish waste tossed overboard from trawlers and other refuse jettisoned out to sea. Some of the birds of the seashore in their turn are preyed on by predators like peregrines, kestrels, harriers, merlins and short-eared owls wintering near the seashore. During the nesting season many eggs, fledgelings and even some adult birds are taken by gulls, crows, foxes, weasels, stoats, rats and other animals, including the polecat in northern Europe.

Tidal beaches in western Europe

Throughout the year, the tidal beaches of the North Sea and Irish Sea, especially near estuaries, produce enormous quantities of animal food. Between them the incoming sea and the outflowing rivers supply this shore zone with colossal amounts of minerals and edible substances of various kinds. The worms, molluscs and crustaceans, which have adapted themselves to the extreme fluctuations in the salt content of the seawater, often occur in large quantities, as do the specialized plants growing on these beaches.

The continental and arctic climate of northeastern Europe forces most bird species to leave during the winter. A large number of ducks, waders and gulls which nest there migrate westwards and southwestwards to western Europe. Many winter in the southern Baltic and the North Sea area, while others continue to the coast of West Africa or even further south. To these birds the animal life of the tidal beaches of western Europe provides a vitally important source of food, at least during part of the year. The importance of the beaches, and the necessity of keeping them free from development and pollution can be more clearly appreciated if the numbers of birds frequenting them are considered. At the peak of the migration period in August, the Waddenzee area in the Netherlands harbours *more than half a million waders.* In some parts of the British Isles, in the Wash or in Morecambe Bay, over 100,000 waders, for example, collect to feed during certain periods of the year.

Many such areas, however, have been partially destroyed, and most are seriously threatened. Many major European cities border on large rivers; pollution, oil discharges, industrial development and even recreational activities are a grave menace to these areas, which are probably indispensable to many bird populations. Ringing surveys indicate that birds winter, or rest and feed during migration, in the same few places year after year.

Field identification and
the outward structure of birds

Field identification techniques have come a long way in the past few decades and are still developing. This is a point well worth underlining, because some currently accepted 'facts' may need to be reconsidered as identification skills improve.

Among the qualities a bird watcher needs are interest, experience, patience and self-criticism. But there is perhaps one which I would particularly like to emphasize – that of 'looking at birds' – really watching and listening to even the most common species. Interest in the rarer species should not blind a bird watcher to the more ordinary ones. A knowledge of variations in the appearance, behaviour, habitats and calls of the most common species is often vitally important when trying to identify a rarer one. Seen in its accustomed surroundings, and in good visibility, a species may be easily recognizable, and you can be certain that it is actually a little stint, a ruff/reeve, a herring gull, a Sandwich tern or whatever. But in every case a multitude of small details of appearance and behaviour can be observed which a small field guide is just not big enough to contain. By watching, and recording your experience in detailed notes, with sketches if possible, you can build your own 'data bank', which will be helpful in identifying rare species and in showing how varied common ones may be.

Because spring in Europe starts in February in the Mediterranean areas, but in June in Scandinavia, the timing of breeding and of plumage changes may vary considerably. Also, the observer must bear in mind that sometimes there is a wide range of individual variation in birds; what you see may not always resemble exactly its description in this book.

When confronted with an unfamiliar bird, for instance a non-European wader belonging to the *Calidris* family, the following questions concerning juvenile little stints may arise: Can the back feathers fall in such a way as to partially conceal the white markings? Could some individuals, due to bleaching or for some other reason, be so pale as to present only a suggestion of reddish brown? Can they give the impression of having a blunt beak? What is their posture while feeding and resting? Are the legs genuinely dark – or perhaps muddy? And so on. All these are characteristics which one has often had the chance of studying, but which vanish without trace if only the species is identified. An important part of the process of bird watching is to make careful field notes of the characteristics observed. This should even be done with reference to birds one recognizes, and notes should always be made of those once cannot identify. Write down all observable characteristics such as behaviour, habitat, accompanying birds, circumstances, time of observation and, in the case of unusual species, the names

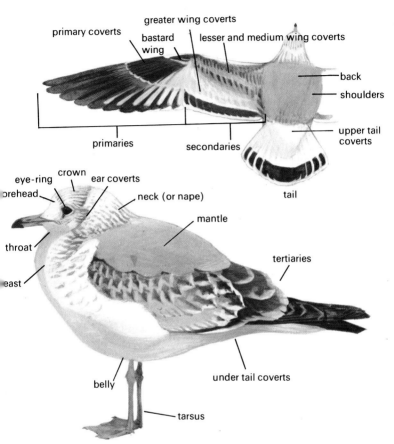

Juvenile – *A bird is a juvenile while it still has its first set of wing feathers, but here, unless otherwise indicated, the designation stands for the first real plumage once the nestling has lost its down.*

Adult – *A bird is adult when it has developed its full mature plumage.*

Subadult – *A bird is subadult (or immature) when it is no longer juvenile but has not yet developed its adult plumage. In larger birds, there may be two or three changes of immature plumage.*

of any co-observers. Drawing a sketch of the bird also helps, because this really forces close study.

When identifying a bird in its natural environment, it may be just one striking feature (like the avocet's beak) that settles its identity, but most often it is the accumulation of a series of characteristics and circumstances. The main elements to be observed are the bird's *appearance*, *behaviour*, *call* and *habitat*.

Two-year-old eider drake
preening its plumage

Plumage

When studying a bird's appearance, a knowledge of the names of the various groups of feathers is essential. The main features which separate birds from other animals are their plumage and ability to fly. Basically there are two kinds of feathers: down and contour. Contour feathers can be divided into, on the one hand, wing and tail coverts and flight feathers, and, on the other, the general body feathers. The latter combine to form a continuous protective surface, with the down as an underlying layer for heat insulation. Wing feathers are of two kinds, primaries and secondaries, depending on their position on the 'hand' (primaries) and 'arm' (secondaries) of the wing. The bases of these large and strong flight feathers (remiges) are protected, and strengthened, by smaller feathers called coverts. Above and below the bases of the tail feathers (retrices) there are similar groups of coverts. The first primary and its coverts are called the alula, or bastard-wing, and are attached to the counterpart of the human thumb. Their task is to act like the flaps in an aircraft wing and prevent unfavourable aerodynamic conditions ('stall') developing on top of the wing. The tail plays a vital part in balance and steering. The feathers grow only in certain strips, called tracts, over the body, but spread to form the outward contours of the bird. These feather names are starting points when describing a bird's plumage, and it is therefore important to remember them. They are shown in the illustrations with the names of other structures or of typical markings.

Moulting

The condition of a bird's feathers is crucial to its chances of survival, and plumage must therefore be constantly maintained. Worn and ragged feathers impair flying proficiency and consequently the ability to find food and escape from enemies, as well as resistance to cold and water. Feathers are constantly under strain which results in deterioration, and they must be replaced at regular intervals. This process – moulting – usually occurs fairly regularly and follows particular, often complicated, sequences. Both the sequence and the number of plumage changes per year vary from one family to another. In the adult bird, with few exceptions, wing and tail feathers change once and body feathers once or twice yearly. In certain groups of birds the different plumages and moulting phases have such a great effect on appearance that field identification is impossible without a knowledge of

Two velvet scoters and, between them, a Steller's eider drake in its first eclipse

them. This applies particularly to many duck species, waders and gulls. However, we lack detailed knowledge of moult in several of the larger species.

Adult *ducks* change body plumage three times a year although three or four plumages can be distinguished in the long-tailed duck. Geese and swans have only one distinguishable plumage because they only moult once a year. Ducks wear, for the greater part of the year, a splendid plumage, replaced for a fairly short period some time during the summer or autumn with a summer or 'eclipse' plumage. The eclipse plumage is always less striking and, more often than not, darker than the magnificent plumage. Drakes in eclipse often resemble their ducks, and the eclipse plumage may be a camouflage device. The drakes usually start moulting before the ducks. The species described here usually shed wing and tail feathers during their eclipse period. Many duck species shed almost all their wing feathers at once so that for a short period they are unable to fly. They can survive because, unlike land birds, they do not depend on their flying ability for food. They often become shy while flightless and certain species, such as all geese, the shelduck and the eider drake, will flock together in suitably sheltered places.

The juvenile plumage (the first real plumage) in most species resembles the summer plumage of the female and like hers is excellent camouflage. The adult plumage, which for diving ducks does not appear until the second or third year, is preceded by a varying number of subadult plumages. These subadult plumages – first winter, first summer, second winter – often display great individual variations. For example, year-old eider drakes may be almost as different in plumage as first-year and second-year birds. The first winter plumage of the drake especially is a potential cause of mistaken identity in many species. For instance, year-old velvet scoter drakes and some older ducks may be confused with Steller's eider drakes because they have no white patch round the eye and little, if any, yellow on their beaks. Year-old eider drakes may be mistaken for king eiders because of their dark backs or year-old scaup drakes can be confused with tufted ducks because they have dark backs and no white at the base of the beak. Geese in their first year can be distinguished from their seniors by their rounder and smaller feathers. This is particularly noticeable on the belly markings.

The appearance of *waders* is drastically affected by the way the feathers wear as well as by occasional old feathers left after moulting. Generally adults have two plumages, one summer and one winter. Summer plumage is acquired by a partial moult (only the body feathers are changed, although the tail feathers, tertiaries and certain wing coverts are shed occasionally) during late winter or spring; the winter plumage by complete moulting (both body and wing feathers) between June and December. The Kentish plover is an exception, with its three annual changes of body plumage. The ruff, too, tends to have three adult plumages: a non-breeding plumage from June–August to February–March and a subsequent incipient spring plu-

Dunlin

Juvenile plumage with winter feathers appearing

Variation of juvenile plumage

Winter plumage

Heavily worn adult summer plumage

Year-old staying on in wintering place, with isolated summer feathers

Fresh adult summer plumage, Siberian race

mage which is filled out later in spring with the well-known ruff at the neck and other highly-coloured feathers.

In most waders the juvenile plumage differs from one of the adult ones, and in colour it often comes midway between the winter and summer plumages of the adults. Between August and January (seldom later) it is exchanged for a winter plumage resembling the adult's, although wing feathers, except tertiaries, are never included and tail feathers are seldom included in this moult. Like the one subsequently leading to the summer plumage, this moult shows great individual variation. The young of many waders often spend their first summer in their wintering areas, when they acquire what is virtually a second winter plumage, but often with elements of adult summer feathers.

The autumn migration period can be very prolonged, and birds often moult during pauses on their journey south. A good example of the effects of wear is the little stint, whose new summer plumage is a not very bright reddish brown. The feathers have pale edges (fringes) which give a scaly impression from a distance. These fringes gradually wear off, and towards June the little stint's plumage is at its reddest. Later in July this redness is lost due to bleaching and wear (cf. the dunlins, p. 17). Since the feathers are replaced successively, the bird's overall appearance constantly changes as new feathers appear. Those observing juvenile dunlins in July will find their backs almost red ochre, while an observer in September will note that they are a light grey-fawn. The beige or red ochre 'touch' so often seen in fresh juvenile specimens of the knot and curlew sandpiper, for instance, often fades relatively quickly.

In *gull* species it is mainly the juvenile and subadult plumages that could pose recognition problems. Non-juveniles shed their body feathers once during the spring and again during summer–autumn. Wing and tail feathers change once yearly during summer–autumn, although there are exceptions. In adult gulls the head and breast display varying dark patches in winter, while species with dark summer heads mainly lose this marking in winter. The juvenile bird changes body feathers only during the first moult (usually summer–autumn), subsequently following the scheme already described, although subadult gulls will often start wing moulting a month or two earlier than adults. The duration of the juvenile stage varies between 12 and 15 months for smaller species like the black-headed gull and kittiwake and up to four years for larger ones like the great black-backed gull and herring gull. The timetable for moulting and the wearing of the different plumages varies greatly, however, between different populations and between individual members of the same population. Malnutrition and hatching times can effectively delay or accelerate the process. A great black-backed gull in its second winter (about 20 months old) need not be wearing its so-called second winter plumage with isolated grey feathers in the mantle; it may still be wearing its 'first' winter plumage, with white and brown mantle markings. Missing wing feathers or those not yet grown out can also influence wing span, wing silhouette and mode of flight. Bleaching often affects the wing appearance of a subadult gull; it pales and loses contrast. For instance, the wing feathers of subadult herring gulls are quite often pale just before they are shed.

In considering colour and markings, therefore, take into account the normal changes occurring in the plumage of the individual bird, which are influenced by *age*, *moulting phase* and *wear*.

Apart from plumage differences between the periods in the life of an individual bird, there are those between separate individuals. Striking differences can be seen in ruffs (p. 76) and skua species (p. 93). Other species which may appear uniform often prove on closer inspection to show considerable variations. Ducks, geese, waders and gulls often exhibit such differences in colour and marking.

Variation in the appearance
of the ringed plover, sketched
on two separate occasions

C. hiaticula tundrae
Neneby, Varanger.
14.6.75 +4°C

C. hiaticula hiaticula
Västergarn, Gotland
21.7.75 +26°C

Shape and size

Shape and size are decisive factors in the field recognition of certain species. When viewed standing on a beach, the different wader species in winter plumage are most easily identified by size, beak shape and length, and leg length. Very often, however, size is hard to assess. Ideally, make a comparison with an accompanying bird whose size is already known. Posture and shape can make a species look larger or smaller than it actually is. The Brent goose, for instance, looks far bigger and heavier than a mallard, although there is little difference between them. Fog makes things look larger than they really are.

Apart from the more obvious differences such as leg length and beak shape, there are also a number of minor differences of posture and shape – neck angle, forehead slope, plumpness and tail angle – which are useful recognition aids. Although body shape and posture vary with what the bird is doing, the small give-away angles making up the bird's 'personality' often remain. There may be quite a difference, however, between body shape in the resting and active states: a wood sandpiper at rest, for instance, hardly seems to have any neck, but in a nervous state it displays a long graceful one.

Birds of all ages fluff out their feathers in cold weather to improve the insulation. But young birds tend to be rounder or fluffier than their elders. This is clearly apparent among juvenile waders, which often seem to be more portly and rounder in the belly than adult birds.

Bird calls

The more one learns about birds the more important their calls become for recognition purposes. Of the species mentioned, it is primarily among geese, waders and gulls that calls play a significant part in identification and discovery. Many related species such as Temminck's stint, little stint, wood sandpiper and green sandpiper are most easily distinguished by their notes when on the wing.

Species frequenting the coast often perform mating and nesting ceremonies involving visual contacts. Calls corresponding to the songs of the passeriformes are often primitive, except for those of the waders, and are seldom uttered without some form of visual display: waders 'sing' while standing with wings raised and ducks call or whistle to the accompaniment of head movements and demonstrations of contrasting colour markings. The notes of each species have a special significance, more closely defined in some cases than others. They can be divided into groups according to function; but the boundaries are often flexible. The real implication may be shown by an inflection or a repetition, or reinforced by a form of behaviour. The following list, therefore, only gives rough guidance: *mating call (song)*, *summoning and contact call, warning call* and *other calls.* Contact and summoning calls also include the *flight call,* by which a bird makes or maintains contact with other members of its species. In many species which migrate in flocks, this contact is usually intensified when landing and taking off. The warning call uttered at nesting places often resembles other calls.

The nest is also defended by other forms of behaviour. Gulls protect their eggs and young by intimidating dive-bombing attacks, ducks and certain wader species divert the attention of the marauder by feigning injury and the ringed plover poses as a fledgeling.

To the category of *other calls* add the various sounds uttered in connection with mating and relief during nesting. The young often have a special call of their own and changeover to the adult call is a gradual process. Young, non-juvenile geese and gulls, for example, can have *intermediate calls.*

Birds of the same species may vary in their calls as well as in appearance. Listen to and write down calls identified. Descriptions and transcriptions of calls are even more dependent on highly individual judgements than descriptions of appearance. Describing, perhaps by means of similes, the various calls and combinations of calls of a species as they strike one personally is very useful.

Behaviour, habitat and distribution

Observing behaviour or general deportment is a good way of deciding to which family a bird belongs. Many relatively similar species differ behaviourally. Therefore, observe how the bird flies and looks for food, whether it occurs in flocks or singly, which part of the shore it prefers and so on. Plovers, for example, are easily distinguished from other waders merely by the characteristic pattern of their movements as a group. The little stint is full of enthusiasm and often runs, indeed almost rolls, over the beach, while Temminck's stint walks, moving far more cautiously, and is often somewhat hunched. Thus a bird's pattern of movement forms part of the general impression.

The silhouette of a bird on the wing can often be identified by the speed of wing movement and trajectory of flight. Both of these, for example, are often very important in the reliable recognition of shearwaters, gannets, storm petrels and gulls.

A bird often frequents special types of shore and only a limited portion of that shore. Spotted redshanks, for instance, often look for food in 10 cm or more of water, while the common sandpiper seldom ventures out into the water.

Geographical distribution is another important clue to identification but cannot be taken as *proof* in itself: consider the *probability* of an observation in relation to the area in which the species normally occurs. But it takes

Blue: nests, occurs during the summer season only
Blue dot: isolated cases of nesting, isolated colony
Blue and shading: nests and winters
Shading: winters
Arrow: principal migration routes

more powerful evidence, good factual documentation and more self-confidence by the observer to identify a bird outside the area in which the species is normally encountered. The incidence of a species at different periods of the year is yet another factor. Each species described in this book is accompanied by a map showing its distribution. A legend explaining the various fields and signs in these maps is shown above.

Population density varies a great deal, and it must be remembered that certain species are exceedingly rare or entirely lacking in large parts of the areas they inhabit. Wintering areas may vary considerably from one year to another but nesting areas are generally more constant. Many species may also be seen during migration at some points outside, but mostly in between, the frequented areas shown on the maps. For example, most of the Arctic waders can be observed on the shores of the Baltic.

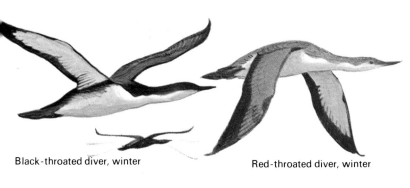

Black-throated diver, winter   Red-throated diver, winter

Divers *Gaviidae*

Their cigar-shaped bodies and strong legs, placed well back, are ideally suited for living in water. They nest on tarns and lakes, but mainly migrate and winter along the sea coasts. The northern boundary of the wintering area for black- and red-throated divers in the Baltic depends on the ice, thus it varies from year to year. Divers live on fish and other small aquatic creatures. Field recognition of the various species is complicated by our incomplete knowledge of their moulting processes and intermediate plumages between juvenile, and winter and summer dress. Also, divers are shy and generally keep well out to sea and when migrating usually fly at a considerable height.

The black- and red-throated divers could be confused with the considerably smaller great crested grebe and red-necked grebe, lake-nesting species also seen along the sea coast in winter. The great crested grebe (*Podiceps cristatus*), 52 cm, is unmistakable in summer with its reddish brown and black frill and ear-like tufts. In winter dress the neck and head are predominantly light in colour, almost a dirty white, broken only by the black crown and pink beak. The bird's silhouette in flight is somewhat similar to the diver's, but its wing beats are much faster and it displays conspicuous white wing markings.

The red-necked grebe (*Podiceps griseigena*), 46 cm, is smaller and squatter. In summer it has a reddish brown neck, grey chin and cheeks and a blackish brown crown. In winter the neck is darker (brownish grey) than the great crested grebe's, with a strikingly pale chin and cheeks and a dark crown. In flight it reveals white wing markings similar to the great crested grebe.

23

Black-throated diver   *Gavia arctica*   58–68 cm

Slightly larger than the red-throated, but far smaller than the great northern and white-billed divers. Nests on deep, clear forests, moorland and mountain lakes but often migrates along the sea coasts. In non-breeding plumage, much darker than the red-throated diver, with dark cheeks, serpentine neck and head, thicker beak and a convex upper mandible. In summer dress has white patches on the back and black chin and throat. It is smaller than the great northern and white-billed divers with dark upper parts and a differently shaped head and neck. The upper parts of young birds are tinged with light brown, giving a somewhat lighter impression from afar, and the beak is paler. On the sea coast, size and colour are uncertain recognition criteria from a distance, except by direct comparison, and the black-throated then may be confused with the great northern and white-billed divers. On the wing it has an unusual flight silhouette (see previous page). Wing beats are slow and strikingly shallow, and its wing tips seem very flexible. In flight the dark sides of the black-throated diver's belly, which form a wide band beneath the wings, are more heavily marked and conspicuous than those of the red-throated diver but in silhouette the two birds are very hard to separate. Also, divers are distinguishable by the distance between the individual birds; ducks fly more closely bunched together. The black-throated diver sits low on the water, and has a smooth, 'semi-somersault' diving technique. The great northern diver sinks straight down.

Red-throated diver   *Gavia stellata*   53–58 cm

Slightly smaller than the black-throated diver. Head and beak are slimmer, head profile squarer and the uptilted beak shape and head angle are also different. The red patch on its throat (summer dress) merely looks dark from a distance. In non-breeding plumage it is much paler than the black-throated, with distinct white spots on the upper part of its body. There is no clear contrast between the crown and nape and the chin and throat. The young are browner, with indistinct grey patches on the upper parts. In flight, the red-throated is not readily distinguishable from the black-throated diver. The wing beats, however, are somewhat deeper and faster. Often seen in small groups, sometimes in sizeable flocks.

Black-throated diver

Red-throated diver

Black-throated diver

summer

winter

Red-throated diver

summer

winter

moulting, spring

White-billed diver

Great northern diver *Gavia immer* 68–81 cm

Nests in Alaska, Canada, Greenland and Iceland (Jan Mayen and Spitsbergen), thus seen further west than the white-billed. The white-billed and great northern divers differ from the black- and red-throated in size and weight, in their shorter and thicker necks and the steep angle between forehead and beak. In flight the great northern is heavy and goose-like. In non-breeding dress it is difficult to distinguish from the white-billed diver, and the shape of its bill, with slightly arched upper mandible like the black-throated, is unreliable for recognition because some individuals have a straight upper mandible. In both species, the young do not acquire beaks of the full length and shape until they are about eight months old. The upper mandible is dark (although the rest of the bill shades from black to light greyish white). The head posture is horizontal (instead of slightly elevated) and the chin and sides of its throat are generally darker. Narrow pale fringes are often clearly perceptible on the back and shoulder feathers of the young great northern, but in the white-billed they are so broad that the bird appears far lighter. In older birds pale markings are thinner and less conspicuous. At close quarters when the bird's wings are fully outstretched the quills of the wing feathers are dark brown in the great northern diver and pale in the white-billed.

White-billed diver *Gavia adamsii* 84–87 cm

A more easterly species than the great northern, it mainly frequents Arctic and Asian areas. The bill varies from yellowish white, horn colour or bluish white to pure white. The upper mandible is no darker, although its base can be a dark horn colour. In the water its head tilts upwards like the red-throated. In non-breeding dress it seems paler than the great northern diver and the head and sides of its throat are lighter. Young birds particularly are very pale (see also above).

Great northern diver

White-billed diver

Great northern diver

juvenile

winter

summer

winter

White-billed diver

summer

Fulmars and Shearwaters   *Procellariidae*

The birds in this group spend most of their lives over the open sea, only visiting land for breeding. The species described here have a characteristic flight: a few swift wing beats followed by long glides with wings held stiff.

Fulmar   *Fulmarus glacialis*   47 cm

The fulmar differs from the shearwaters in its outwardly similar appearance to gulls, and from gulls by its characteristic flight – a straight glide on stiff, straight wings, interspersed with short bursts of wing beats. Often observed far out to sea, it nests in colonies on cliff faces and crags not necessarily close to the sea. It sometimes nests on old buildings or even on new coastal power stations. In nesting places it will emit nasal grunts and cacklings. Its diet is animals, dead or alive, found close to the surface of the sea.

Manx shearwater   *Puffinus puffinus*   35 cm

The most common shearwater species in the North Atlantic and North Sea. Striking contrast between near-black upper and white lower parts of the body. Gentle flight with long glides and rapid, flapping wing beats. There are three races in Europe, two in the Mediterranean. The westernmost (*mauretanicus*) occasionally frequents the coasts of western Europe in autumn. The upper part of the body is sooty grey and the lower part dirty white, with dark shading over the flanks. The much smaller (27 cm long) but very similar little shearwater (*Puffinus assimilis*) nests on some islands off the northwest African coast and is very occasionally found in the North Atlantic as far as southwestern Ireland. It has faster, more fluttering wing beats and glides for shorter stretches than the Manx. The Manx shearwater often occurs in flocks, sometimes in huge numbers. Around a shoal of fish, the feeding flock advances with a characteristic 'rolling' movement; the birds at the rear fly forward in a steady stream and take the lead. They breed in colonies, in holes burrowed in steep grassy slopes or in rocky screes on marine islands, occasionally at a great height above sea level. They usually visit their nesting sites only at night, when they make cackling and wailing sounds. Their diet is mainly fish.

Fulmar

Manx shearwater

Fulmar

dark phase   light phase

Manx shearwater

Great shearwater *Puffinus gravis* 46 cm

Breeds during the northern hemisphere winter in Tristan da Cunha and Gough Island in the South Atlantic, then migrates north along the American coast and later southwards during our summer and autumn, off the coasts of western Europe and Africa. Irregularly seen in western Europe, although in some years it appears in considerable numbers. Much bigger than the Manx shearwater, the dark crown, light band around the neck and light brown upper part of the body are the best distinguishing marks. The pale tips of the upper tail coverts often stand out clearly, especially in strong light. Its flight is rapid, reminiscent of the fulmar. Could be confused with Cory's shearwater (*Calonectris diomedea*), which is slightly larger (46–50 cm), has a paler, more evenly-coloured grey head, greyish brown upper body and a bright horn-yellow bill. Cory's shearwater regularly visits the Bay of Biscay but seldom further north. Both species live mostly on small fish and the larger zoo plankton near the sea surface.

Sooty shearwater *Puffinus griseus* 42 cm

Rarely but regularly visits the South Atlantic, recognized by the uniformly dark, sooty grey colour, cigar-shaped body and comparatively slender wings. Can be confused with dark phase skuas, but these have a longer tail and pale patches at the base of the primaries. The light patches underneath the wings are often only visible at close quarters; at a distance it appears completely dark. Small numbers seen mostly during the summer and autumn along the coasts of western Europe.

below
Manx shearwater

Opposite page, top to bottom
Great shearwater
Sooty shearwater
Fulmar

Storm petrel

Leach's petrel

Storm petrel · *Hydrobates pelagicus* · 15 cm

A sooty-black sea bird with a white rump, it flies low over water with fast, jerky wing beats. Could be confused with Leach's petrel (below) or the similar Wilson's petrel (*Oceanites oceanicus*), which visits the waters off the coasts of southwestern Europe from its Antarctic breeding grounds. Wilson's petrel has larger pale patches in the wing coverts, darker than those of the Leach's petrel, yellow webs between its toes, longer legs and completely dark underwings. Its flight is even more fluttery and it often patters on the water surface with legs dangling and wings uplifted. Both species follow ships. The storm petrel nests in holes or rock crevices on marine islands. It is active around its breeding grounds during the night. From the nesting holes there are long drawn-out rising and falling purring sounds, interspersed at regular intervals with repeated short, sharp whistles – 'tchwee'. It mostly feeds on plankton plucked straight from the water's surface in flight.

Leach's petrel · *Oceanodroma leucorrhoa* · 20 cm

Bigger than the storm petrel but with a longer-winged silhouette, a jerkier, more nervously bounding flight and sudden, bat-like changes of direction. Soft greyish brown. At close quarters, the slightly forked tail, the white rump with a dark central stripe and the pale wing coverts are clearly visible. The wings are dark underneath. This species rarely accompanies ships. From nesting holes successions of varied purring sounds, 'wirra-wirra', and whistles are interspersed with hiccough-like noises. Nesting and feeding are similar to the storm petrel.

Storm petrel

Leach's petrel

Gannet

juvenile

subadult

adult

Gannet *Sula bassana* 91 cm

Old and subadult birds are unmistakable in size, colour and pattern. Juveniles have a cigar-shaped body, long pointed tail, long wings and characteristic movements. Not to be confused with one of the albatross species (rarely observed in the North Atlantic, but usually the black-browed *Diomedea melanophrys*). Adult plumage develops in slow stages until the fifth year. The yellow ochre of the head is paler outside the breeding season. A majestic bird, it is an expert diver, sometimes dropping from over 100 feet. They are silent at sea, but in the breeding grounds they emit high-pitched goose-like croaks. They nest in colonies, sometimes tens of thousands strong, on rock stacks and islands and on ledges of vertical nesting cliffs. Fish diet.

adult
Cormorant

juvenile

Shag

Cormorant *Phalacrocorax carbo*   90 cm

A big, dark, somewhat reptilian water bird. On land it sits upright, spreading its wings after swimming, as it lacks efficient waterproofing oils. Groups often stand on rock ledges and stones a short way from shore. Swims low in the water, with long slender neck held straight up and head tilted slightly upwards. Cormorants fly in a straight, purposeful trajectory with quite slow wing beats. A characteristic feature in flight is the head held a little higher than the body. May be confused with the shag, especially younger birds, which are quite variable and can have a completely brownish plumage with no more than a pale throat shading. Young birds have pale bellies, but the cormorant is altogether larger, has a thicker neck, head and bill and more leisurely wing beats than the shag. There is no white patch across the thigh in non-breeding plumage. The continental race (*sinensis*, breeding in the Baltic) has a very conspicuous white fringe around its neck for a short period during the nesting season. This race builds nests of twigs in trees, while the Atlantic race (*carbo*) breeds on cliff ledges or low islets. The cormorant lives on fish.

Shag *Phalacrocorax aristotelis*   76 cm

Smaller and slimmer than the cormorant, with a short neck, smaller head, thinner beak and faster wing beats. Older birds only have crests for a short period at the beginning of the nesting season. The young have no pale markings – or, in rare cases, very few – on the belly, and at close quarters they have pointed back feathers (cf. the cormorant). Shags nest in small groups on cliff ledges, often under boulders, and are a common sight on the North Atlantic bird cliffs.

Cormorant

Shag

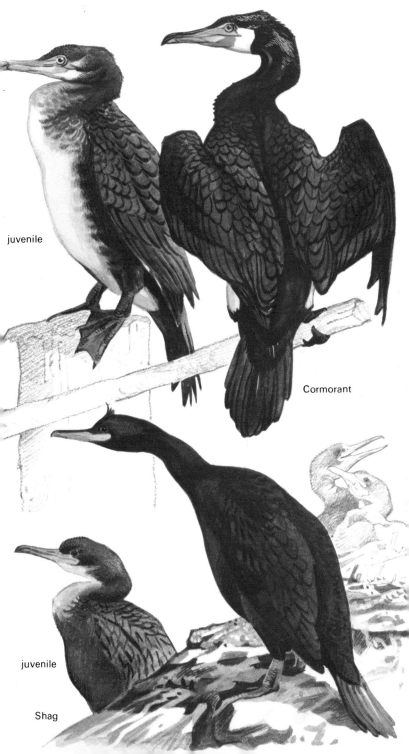

juvenile

Cormorant

juvenile

Shag

Ducks *Anatidae*

All duck species can swim and feed in the water. They have webbed feet, long bodies with dense, highly waterproof plumage over a thick layer of down, and long necks. Wing feathers are shed annually, such a rapid process that they cannot fly for a short period. Ducks, mergansers, goosanders and smews have a magnificent plumage for most of the year and an eclipse dress for a short period during the summer and early autumn (see also p. 14). The young are downy, and can swim and find their own food soon after they are hatched. Ducks are divided into the following groups.

Swans (sub-family *Cygninae*).

Geese (sub-family *Anserinae*). Except for the greylag goose, European geese breed in northern or Arctic latitudes, wintering in large flocks in open coastal meadows or fields further inland. They graze mainly on shore plants but some eat cereals and potatoes. Highly gregarious, they often spend the winter in large flocks of more than one species. Comparisons of size and profile often aid recognition.

Dabbling ducks (*Anatinae*). A group found mainly in fresh water. Near the sea they occur mostly on estuaries or brackish lagoons. In some places, however (especially around the Baltic, which has a very low salt content), the mallard, pintail, wigeon and teal occur fairly regularly close to the seashore. Only the shelduck, a close relative of the dabbling ducks, is included here (p. 46), as it is primarily associated with the seashore. A dabbling duck characteristic is to graze on submerged vegetation by 'up-ending' its body vertically in the water and stretching its neck down to the bottom. They obtain food by filtering small creatures out of the surface water or soft mud with their beaks. Take-off is a jump straight out of the water (cf. diving ducks).

Diving ducks (*Aythyinae*) dive for their food. They take to the wing by running with wings flapping.

 Smaller diving ducks. Mostly ducks confined to fresh water, although several species can occur fairly regularly along some seashores. Apart from scaup (p. 50) it is mostly goldeneye (*Bucephala clangula*) and tufted duck (*Aythya fuligula*) that are seen by the sea.

 Larger diving ducks. These are mainly marine species, although the long-

Goldeneye   ♂   Tufted duck   ♂

tailed duck, common scoter and velvet scoter breed beside mountain lakes. The identification of young birds of the eider species is difficult because their appearance varies a great deal (see p. 15, moulting ducks). Like the smew, red-breasted merganser and goosander they live mainly on animal food, such as mussels and other molluscs, crustaceans and marine worms.

Two diving duck species occur in Iceland, Barrow's goldeneye (*Bucephala islandica*) and harlequin (*Histrionicus histrionicus*). Both breed near fresh water but are seen off the seashore in winter. The *Merginae* (smew, red-breasted merganser and goosander), with their long, narrow, serrated bills, are adept at catching live fish. Like diving ducks, they patter along the surface before take-off.

Because ducks can show great individual plumage variations and are often seen in silhouette at sea, head and beak shapes are useful criteria in field recognition. At the top, left to right: three velvet scoters and a common scoter duck. Centre: year-old king eider drake and an adult duck. Bottom: two eider ducks and a year-old drake.

Whooper swan *Cygnus cygnus* 152 cm

The call, noisy habits, yellow bill base and straighter neck make it different from the mute swan. Distinguished from Bewick's swan by its considerably larger size, longer neck, more elongated head, greater expanse of yellow on the bill (which varies between birds) and its call. The young are a more even shade of grey than young mute swans with fewer dark bill markings. Youngsters are almost invariably accompanied by adult birds. The whooper makes loud trumpeting notes in various nasal timbres – 'hwang', 'clong' etc. – often heard in V-formation flights. It is found in freshwater lakes, rivers or shallow bays. The northern boundary of its wintering area depends on the ice. Mainly lives on water-weeds, but tends to graze on grassland like geese more often than the mute swan.

Bewick's swan *Cygnus bewickii* 122 cm

Has a smaller yellow area on its bill than the whooper swan, which, from a distance, makes it appear almost completely dark. Its call, shape and size are also different. Except when direct comparison is available, size cannot normally be used for identification, and the plumper body, shorter neck and rounder head are also difficult to gauge. A more goose-like call than the whooper swan's, with a barking 'haw ... haw, haw'. Winters by the seashore and nearby lakes. Same diet as the whooper swan.

Mute swan *Cygnus olor* 152 cm

Distinguished by the black knob at the bill base, soft S-shaped neck curve and frequently arched or 'inflated' wings. In flight the wings make a distinctive and melodious swishing sound, quite loud, which is not produced by the whooper swan. The young resemble adults but are browner with dark nostrils and a dark area at the bill base. Common on inland waters, and the seashore, mostly in winter, but also breeds extensively around the Baltic shores.

Red-breasted goose *Branta ruficollis* 53–56 cm

Breeds locally on the Arctic coast of Siberia and winters mainly in the USSR, although a small number winter in southeastern Europe. Very rarely, a few are observed among the Siberian barnacle geese wintering in the North Sea area (see illustration, p. 40).

Whooper swan

Bewick's swan

Mute swan

juvenile

Whooper swan

juvenile

Bewick's swan

Mute swan   Whooper swan   Bewick's swan

Brent geese

Brent goose *Branta bernicla*   56–61 cm

Barely larger than a mallard drake, but its goose-shaped body and behaviour make it look bigger. At a distance, a flock on the wing can be taken for barnacle geese or eider duck. Two races, *hrota*, nesting in Greenland and Spitsbergen, and *bernicla*, nesting in Siberia, winter in large flocks on western European coasts. The eastern-most race is much darker underneath, with young birds giving a very dark overall impression. At first the young do not have the white patch on the throat. They have pale-edged wing coverts which give their wings a striped appearance. Their call is a nasal, mumbling, 'crraut, crraut'. Migration is somewhat earlier in the autumn and later in the spring than for barnacle geese. Small skeins often fly in a straggling line. Lives mainly on eel grass (*Zostera*), thus closely attached to the sea.

Barnacle goose *Branta leucopsis*   58–69 cm

Has somewhat longer wings and is noisier in the air than the Brent. When migrating, constantly makes short 'barks'. The Canada goose (*Branta canadensis*), which also has white cheeks and was originally introduced into Europe, is at least one and a half times larger than the barnacle goose, with a predominantly brown plumage instead of grey. Unlike the Brent goose, which mainly frequents the polar regions, it breeds only in Novaya Zemlya, Spitsbergen and parts of eastern Greenland. The entire world population makes the autumn migration to the British Isles and the North Sea areas for the winter. Grazes on various grasses from seashore, fields and meadows.

Brent goose

Barnacle goose

Red-breasted goose

juvenile

adult

Brent goose,
dark-bellied race

Barnacle goose   juvenile

White-fronted goose

Greylag goose

White-fronted goose *Anser albifrons* 66–76 cm

Distinguished from all other species except the lesser white-fronted goose by a white patch around the bill base and black bars on its breast. Compared with the lesser white-fronted, the white patch at the bill base is smaller and the bright yellow rings around its eyes are lacking, although it may have greyish fawn ones. It is larger, and more closely resembles the greylag goose. Young birds lacking the white patch at the bill base and dark breast markings differ from the greylag and bean goose by their beak colour. Young birds are nearly always accompanied by their elders. The white patch at the bill base appears during the first winter, and the black bars on the breast develop during the second autumn. The Greenland race (*flavirostris*), which winters in western Scotland and in Ireland, has an orange beak, somewhat longer and thicker than the Siberian race (*albifrons*). In flight the white-fronted looks longer in the wing and shorter in the neck than the bean goose. Its call is a variable 'cao-yoo', while on the wing it has a melodius 'kiu-kiock', more high-pitched than the bean goose's.

Lesser white-fronted goose – see p. 44.

Greylag goose *Anser anser* 76–89 cm

Distinguished by striking wing markings in flight, and a bright yellow or pink bill with a white tip. The eastern races (*rubrirostris*), which breed beside lakes in eastern Europe and further east, have pink beaks and paler upper parts. The greylags breeding in the Baltic, however, include some with predominantly pink bills. Noisy, with a nasal, resonant but sometimes harsh cackling sound similar to the farmyard goose. Its thick neck and head make it look heavy in flight. The lesser wing coverts are paler than in other geese. Prefers to breed on lonely islets and peninsulas or beside lakes with abundant vegetation.

White-fronted goose

Greylag goose

juvenile

Greenland

Siberian
White-fronted goose

Lesser white-fronted goose

eastern

western

Greylag goose

Bean goose

Pink-footed goose

Lesser white-fronted goose *Anser erythropus*   53–66 cm

Smaller, rounder and squatter than the white-fronted, with a round head, shorter neck, short stubby bill and a yellow ring around each eye. Its call is harsher and higher-pitched.

Bean goose *Anser fabalis*   71–89 cm

Looks browner than the greylag. Its neck and head are conspicuously dark, its neck is longer, head narrower and beak longer and marked with black. In flight its wings show pale, less striking markings than the greylag's, but because the colour of the upper parts can be hard to judge on wing, the longer neck and oblong head are important distinguishing characteristics, apart from its 'hoink-hoink' call. Bill markings vary, and some also have a pale ring around the base (see below).

Pink-footed goose *Anser brachyrhynchus*   67–76 cm

Differs from the bean goose by much paler grey upper parts, the flanks being the darkest body area, by its shorter neck, rounder head and much shorter, stubby, pink and black bill and pink legs. Juveniles are browner and slightly drabber than the bean goose, and during their first autumn their legs vary between yellow-fawn and greyish pink. When seen with bean goose on the wing the pink-foot is smaller, shorter in the neck, and its upper parts are lighter grey. Bill colour, silhouette and call distinguish it from the greylag. The pink-foot is the noisiest of all the goose species: its calls are generally in a higher key than the bean goose's.

Lesser white-fronted goose

Bean goose

Pink-footed goose

Bean geese

Bean goose

Pink-footed goose

Eider ♀

Shelduck

Eider ♂

Shelduck   *Tadorna tadorna*   ♂ 61–71 cm   ♀ 54–59 cm

The adult is unmistakable but the young are drab. During their moult, often congregate on suitable expanses of sandbanks. During the breeding season they put on a series of striking displays in which they chase each other, flaunt the chestnut band across their breast, preen and wag their heads. The drake has a whistling call, the duck a noisier, quacking 'ga-ga-ga-ga-ga-ga-gak'. Common on mudflats, bays and estuaries. Also found on freshwater lakes near the sea, and surprisingly often in fields far away from the sea where the shelduck will usually be looking for a suitable nesting place. Lives on snails, worms, larvae and small quantities of grain and grass shoots.

Eider   *Somateria mollissima*   59–67 cm

Likely to be confused with the mallard or one of the two Arctic eider species. Ducks and drakes in eclipse and in their first and second winter dresses are particularly hard to distinguish from king eiders (see pp. 15 and 16 and, for the king eider, p. 48). The eider duck is large and squat, with an endearing 'motherly' and somewhat 'elderly' expression. Like dabbling ducks, eiders sometimes 'up-end' when looking for food on the seabed near the seaweed of the shoreline. Most drakes leave the breeding grounds soon after the ducks start incubating. They then moult in large flocks out at sea. During the mating process the drake utters a loud, emphatic 'ah-haóh' and the duck a clucking 'cock-ock-ock-ock ...' Feeds mostly on mussels, while the young subsist on crustaceans from near the water's edge.

Shelduck

Eider

venile

♀

♂

Shelduck

year-old ♂

♂

♀

Eider

two-year-old ♂

♀

♂

♀

King eider ♂

Steller's eider

King eider *Somateria spectabilis* 55–62 cm

The adult drake in its magnificent dress is unmistakable. The first-year drake always has the hint of a knob at the bill base; this is orange, or possibly a greyish pink and has a dark surround. The back of the head is round. In second-year plumage the drake usually displays many features of the adult dress. In its first- and second-year plumages, the eider drake has a much longer bill which is always a dirty fawn or a light grey-green. The eclipse dress of the king eider may be sooty black but often it has touches of white or fawn. The king eider duck varies in colour but is generally redder than the eider although she is more greyish fawn in her first plumage. Compared with the eider she has a shorter bill, rounder head and often a quite distinct 'smile' at the bill base. Very rare in southern and western Europe.

Steller's eider *Polysticta stelleri* 45–49 cm

The drake in breeding plumage is easily recognizable. In first-year plumage and in eclipse dress, the head is strikingly angular, with the neck and crown at right angles. The bill looks rather stout with a perfectly straight vertical base. Old ducks in breeding plumage are very dark, reddish brown-black, and in flight reveal conspicuous white wing-bars and blue wing speculum. On the water the greyish purple and white rear edges of the tertiaries and secondaries show clearly. Some ducks have distinct pale rings around their eyes. Their flight is rapid, with fast, slightly swishing wing beats. In winter lives mainly on molluscs and crustaceans. This species often occurs in large flocks in the north, but is very rare in southern and western Europe. Very few winter in the Baltic.

King eider

Steller's eider

King eider

♀

Eider ♀

ar-old ♂

♂

year-old ♂

♀

Steller's eider

♂

Scaup *Aythya marila*

48 cm

Sometimes found in winter together with the tufted duck (p. 36). In mixed flocks scaup are distinguished by the brilliant white patch around the female's bill. Female tufted ducks have a narrower white 'bridle' but never display such a striking expanse of white as the duck scaup. The female scaup's greyer mantle and the grey back of the drake are noted in winter. (Tufted drakes preening themselves and turning belly-up can give the illusion of having the light back of the scaup.) In juvenile and eclipse dress, the scaup's rounder head and wider bill distinguishes it from the tufted duck. The scaup breeds in northern Europe, visiting the south and west only in the winter, which is spent by the sea, on nearby lakes and occasionally on reservoirs and inland lakes.

Velvet scoter *Melanitta fusca*

48–56 cm

Has pale facial patches, a 'longnosed' head shape and white wing patches. Some females do not have light head markings. Around the Baltic they often breed a short distance away from the seashore, on the edge of a wood or forest or under a bush, while further north they nest beside the lakes of the tundra and mountain regions. In southern and western Europe, a regular winter visitor offshore, but much less numerous than the common scoter. Lives on mussels, other molluscs and various crustaceans and often ventures closer to the shore than the common scoter when looking for food.

Common scoter *Melanitta nigra*

43–52 cm

Differs from the velvet scoter by its lack of white wing markings. It is also smaller and much rounder, and from afar the drake has so little yellow on its beak that it looks dark grey. Because of her pale cheeks, the duck looks from a distance as if she has a dark cap. The common scoter breeds on moorland and tundra lakes, but spends the rest of the year out to sea, where non-breeding birds spend the whole year. Often it stays a long way from the shore. It flies quickly, low over the sea, and a flock on the wing often assumes the characteristic formation of a cluster with a straggling 'tail'. Drakes utter soft whistling notes, 'pyu' or 'pyoo-pyoo'. The common scoter lives off the sea and mostly eats mussels, but its diet may include other molluscs, ragworms and crustaceans.

Scaup

Velvet scoter

Common scoter

♀ winter

♀ spring

♂

Scaup

♀

Velvet scoter

♀

♂

♂

♂ Common scoter

vet scoter ♂ ♀

♂

♀

Common scoter

Long-tailed duck   *Clangula hyemalis*   ♂ 58–60 cm   ♀ 37–41 cm

Undergoes complex plumage changes, and ducks in particular show great individual variation. In winter, when some stay out to sea others may come close inshore, even into harbours. The drake is easily recognized by his pale plumage and long tail. During the breeding season the drake has a dark brown upper body, and a black neck and head except for a big light patch around the eye. The duck, with her small stature, short bill and dark cheek markings does not resemble any other European duck except possibly the female harlequin (see p. 37), although some are very pale with only light shading on the cheek and drab greyish brown upper parts. In flight the combination of pale body and dark, long, somewhat curved wings is characteristic. The drake utters a soft but clearly audible 'au – au-li'. During winter the long-tailed duck lives mainly on molluscs and crustaceans. It breeds in mountains and tundra lakes.

Red-breasted merganser   *Mergus serrator*   51–62 cm

More tied to the sea in winter than the goosander. Breeds on large lakes and clear, fast-flowing rivers in mountain areas. The smooth colour gradation between head and neck, the thinner, less tapered bill and stragglier crests distinguish ducks and drakes in eclipse from the goosander. The merganser nests on the ground, often under vegetation or in a cavity near water, and lives mainly on fish.

Goosander   *Mergus merganser*   58–72 cm

Breeds and winters mainly in fresh water, often on reservoirs well inland, but may be found offshore especially where there are stony or rocky beaches. The duck's body looks grey (with touches of orange in the underparts during winter), the dark reddish brown head contrasting clearly. The ample 'mane' makes the head look kite-shaped in flight. Nests in hollow trees by fast-flowing rivers and lives on fish.

Smew   *Mergus albellus*   Not illustrated   41 cm

Breeds beside fresh water in coniferous forests of northern Europe. It winters mostly in fresh water, but can be seen offshore and in estuaries. It is a small, short-billed bird. The drake is unmistakable, mainly white with a narrow black bill, two vertical black lines down the sides of its breast, watery grey flanks, a black patch round the eye and a white crest. The duck and drake in eclipse are grey with a reddish brown cap and white cheeks. Unusual in Britain in winter; mostly seen on reservoirs.

Long-tailed duck

Red-breasted merganser

Goosander

♀ winter

♀

♂

♂ winter
Long-tailed duck

♂

♀
Goosander

♀

Red-breasted
merganser

♂

Red-breasted merganser

♀

♂

Goosander

Adult bird, Baltic

Predators

68–97 cm

White-tailed eagle *Haliaeetus albicilla* wing span 199 239 cm

An old adult white-tailed eagle ('old' being more than 4–5 years), with its faded plumage, is virtually unmistakable. Juvenile and subadult birds, however, may be confused with other large raptors. Their size, broad solid wing span, wedge-shaped tail, protruding but relatively small head with its formidable beak, frequently pale markings of the 'armpits' (coarser and more conspicuous in subadult birds) and level horizontal gliding posture of the wings are characteristics that distinguish younger white-tailed eagles from the golden and spotted eagles. Subadult white-tailed eagles with plumage in the process of changing into the paler adult dress often present a surprisingly patchy, piebald appearance. Unlike other eagle species, the white-tailed eagle is not an acrobat, but calmly circles at high altitudes. It breeds in northern Norway on cliff ledges, but around the Baltic nests in trees on wooded archipelago islands, and further inland it settles in undisturbed forests and woodlands close to lakes and big rivers. In winter it also frequents open country – fields, meadows and lakes. Most of the older birds are year-round residents, while the younger ones lead a more roving life. The call is a harsh 'kee-ick, kee-ick, kee-ick . . .'

The numbers of white-tailed eagles have declined steeply in this century as a result of deliberate extermination and pollution of the environment. The British population became extinct in the 19th century, but attempts are now being made to re-establish a population on a remote island nature reserve. Because of this, there may now be more sightings in western and southern Europe, where previously the white-tailed eagle has been exceedingly rare. In recent years pollution control measures in the breeding areas may have led to a limited improvement, but the future of the white-tailed population is very uncertain. The main foods are fish, sea birds, and carrion of all kinds. It is a somewhat clumsy hunter, and quite often intercepts ospreys and gulls and robs them of their prey.

subadult

juvenile

White-tailed eagle

adult

juvenile

Grey plover

adult

Peregrine falcon   *Falco peregrinus*   ♂ 39–42 cm   ♀ 49–50 cm

There are many different races of peregrine in different parts of the world, breeding not only by the coast but also in mountains and moorland areas, beside lakes, and even in deserts. The coastal birds nest mainly on steep cliffs. They often spend the winter near estuaries, coastal marshes or other places with an abundance of sea birds. Their plumage is quite variable, especially the colouring of the upper parts, and, like other birds of prey, the female is noticeably larger than the male. A striking feature often seen in older birds is the contrast between the dark bars on the lower parts and the dark head with the paler areas of both breast and head. Of the falcons likely to be seen along the coast of northwestern Europe (peregrine, merlin, kestrel, gyr falcon), the peregrine is most likely to be confused with the gyr falcon, which occurs on the coasts of Norway and Iceland but is much less frequently seen further south. Compared with this species the peregrine is smaller, has a shorter tail, shorter, more pointed wings, far more conspicuous 'moustaches' and faster and deeper wing beats. The flight of the peregrine is confident and elegant, featuring both glides and plunging dives (stoops) in pursuit of prey, with the wings retracted. Like the white-tailed eagle, the peregrine population has been heavily depleted in Europe, due to pollution and human disturbance, although the species is also still being hard hit by egg collectors and falconers taking young birds for training. Lives on birds up to the size of a mallard. Often its presence is first made known by the agitation it causes among nearby birds. On its breeding grounds the peregrine emits a sharp 'ka-yak', and its warning cry is a shrill 'kek-kek-kek-kek'.

Peregrine falcon

juvenile

adult ♂

juvenile

Waders

Waders belong to the order Charadriiformes, which also includes gulls and auks. They are customarily divided into five families: oystercatchers, plovers, phalaropes, avocets and a motley group comprising snipe, godwits, sandpipers and other waders of the *Calidris* and *Limicola* families. A common characteristic is their adaptation to life near the water. Many have long legs and bills which enable them to subsist on the abundant animal life of the seashore, including molluscs, worms, crustaceans and insects. Beaks are shaped according to their various hunting methods (see p. 9).

Most species are migratory, and many breed exclusively in Arctic areas. Some, such as the lapwing and the southern dunlin, migrate for short distances only, while others, such as the curlew sandpiper and ruff, may migrate far south in the southern hemisphere. Many species display an autumn migration graph with two peaks because older birds often migrate from the breeding grounds ahead of the young ones.

Mixed flocks of waders are a common feature during migration, which makes recognition more difficult. Also, most species have three plumages and complicated transitional forms during their moulting periods (see opposite page and p. 17). Apart from the plumage and specific wing and tail markings (e.g. wing bars), the body shape and posture and general behaviour on the wing are important recognition criteria. Calls are another crucial characteristic; each species usually has a distinct vocabulary, with the waders tending to be highly vociferous.

Europe also provides habitats for the woodcock, snipe, jack snipe and great snipe, four species mostly encountered near fresh water. The snipe (*Gallinago gallinago*), 26–28 cm, the most numerous and widespread, can be seen in many areas from inland sewage farms and wet fields to muddy creeks. Distinctive features are the long straight bill, speckled brown upper parts with wide pale stripes, its shy behaviour and its zig-zag flight when disturbed. The terek sandpiper (*Xenus cinereus*), is a rare species whose European breeding grounds lie mostly in the USSR. Several wader species breeding in North America and a small number from Asia are very occasionally seen in Europe – mostly in the west – during the summer and autumn. Of these the pectoral sandpiper (*Calidris melanotos*) is the most regular visitor (see p. 89).

The varying plumages and complex moult of the waders result in great individual differences. Top: two bar-tailed godwits, male in summer dress on the left and a juvenile male on the right. Below: a grey plover in summer dress. Top centre: juvenile sanderlings, on the left changing into winter plumage. Next, four dunlins, showing, left to right, a juvenile changing to winter plumage, an adult in summer dress, juvenile plumage and a sleeping juvenile. At the bottom: a little stint in juvenile dress.

Oystercatcher

Lapwing

Oystercatcher *Haematopus ostralegus* 43 cm

With its striking appearance and call, it steals the ornithological show on many beaches. Young birds and adults in winter have a white 'chinstrap'. Frequents most types of seashore and in northern Britain also ventures far inland. With the redshank and the lapwing it is one of the most vigilant watchdogs of the seashore; an insistent warning note, a shrill 'pick, pick . . .' or 'kubik, kubik . . .' will betray and pester every intruder. Oystercatchers also hold frequent noisy 'kubik' sessions among themselves: the males gather in peculiar meetings at which they troop around, heads down, emitting calls which alternate between vocal hammerings and long trills.

Lapwing *Vanellus vanellus* 30 cm

Always easy to recognize, the most striking of its many unmistakable features is the rounded black and white wings when in flight. Young birds have hardly any crest and the upper parts of their bodies are a 'scaly' golden brown. Adults acquire a similar winter dress between August and November, with a pale chin and throat and scaly upper parts. In many places along the coast, and inland, the lapwing is very common, especially well-known for its springtime aerobatics. In its breeding grounds it emits persistent, plaintive cries of 'pee-wit' or 'vew-vee' but the actual sound varies a great deal. During courtship flight the male 'moans' incessantly and produces a loud buzzing sound with his rounded wings. The lapwing is highly gregarious for most of the year. Meadows, cereal fields and tussocky coastal marshes are favoured breeding grounds, but during migration it can be seen on most kinds of flat shores, pastures and arable fields. At the northern and eastern extremes of its range it is a summer visitor only.

Oystercatcher

Lapwing

Oystercatcher

juvenile

adult

venile

♂

Lapwing

Ringed plover *Charadrius hiaticula* 19 cm

The most common plover species easily recognizable in summer dress by the colour of its legs and beak. Juvenile birds are best distinguished from the little ringed plover by white wing bars and from the Kentish plover by more complete collars and pale reddish legs. When juvenile plumage is still fresh, their upper parts are 'scaly', but the cream-coloured edges of their feathers wear away so that this dress, retained for their first winter, begins to resemble the adult's winter dress. The typical 'too-pip' call is somewhat anxiously articulated but gentle in tone. During mating flight they produce a humming, yodelling 'tack-aly, tack-aly, tack-aly ...'

Little ringed plover *Charadrius dubius* 15 cm

Mud-coloured legs, yellow rings around the eyes, and dark bill, although the base of the lower mandible is often yellow. Call and lack of wing bars are the most distinguishing features. Juvenile has a uniformly drab head without the white patch behind the eye, but with a light semi-circle below the eye and more often than not a yellowish throat and patch on its forehead (although the latter can vary in extent and form a wedge extending over/behind the eye). Flight call is a typical 'peeyoo'. On its breeding grounds emits a loud, desolate-sounding call, starting with a rolling, tern-like piercing 'krrey-krrey ...' Breeds in open areas such as gravel pits, quarries and refuse dumps. During migration it can be observed at lakesides, and on muddy estuary creeks.

Kentish plover *Charadrius alexandrinus* 16 cm

Heavy wear and bleaching makes this species vary a great deal in colour and pattern. Also an additional change of body feathers from the normal two for waders. In all plumages the best guide to identity is the overall impression. Adult birds, at least, are squatters or adopt a more crouching posture than the two plover species mentioned above. They are always a very pale colour, with a stout dark bill and dark legs. Young birds have grey legs. The wide wing bar distinguishes them from the little ringed plover. The male has a red-ochre crown during spring and early summer only. The call is similar to the sanderling, shorter than the ringed plover, a slightly falling 'poo-epp' or 'prree-ip'. Also emits a harsher, more protracted 'prrui', especially during courtship. Found on sandy beaches with extensive shallows and, in southern Europe and Asia, near salt pans.

Ringed plover

Little ringed plover

Kentish plover

Ringed plover

winter

juvenile

juvenile

juvenile

Little ringed plover

♂ spring

Kentish plover

Grey plover *Pluvialis squatarola* 28 cm

Summer plumage lacks the greenish yellow shades of the golden plover, but the females, especially year-olds, often look brownish on top (cf. golden plover). In flight, juveniles and birds in the similar but somewhat duller winter dress display black armpits and a white rump, features distinguishing them from golden plovers. Unlike the golden plover, the grey often occurs singly and is mainly a coastal bird when migrating. It moves in typical 'plover style' (see p. 9). Its call is a loud plaintive bi- or tri-syllabic 'plu-eh' or 'plu-ee-yeh'. A single migrating bird often announces its approach at a considerable distance with this loud whistling call. Along the wide tidal beaches of western Europe, the grey plover is one of the typical birds of passage during the autumn. Most continue further south, sometimes wintering as far away as the coast of South Africa, but many winter on British and Irish estuaries and bays.

Golden plover *Pluvialis apricaria* 27 cm

Back marked with a distinct shade of gold. Pied underparts vary in summer, usually less pronounced in females and most conspicuous in the race breeding in the Arctic. The dark belly is framed by white flanks, unlike the grey plover. Usually flies in flocks and, unlike the grey plover, avoids the immediate shoreline when looking for food, so the two species are seldom found together. In flight, which is fast and straight, the armpits show white and the wings have a very faint bar. The flight call, a monosyllabic whistling 'pee', is more plaintive than that of the grey plover. On their nesting grounds a pair of golden plovers will lament with a fateful 'plu-i-vie', the male contributing rhythmically repeated sequences. The southern race breeds on mossy moorland and rocky plateaus. During migration, seen on coastal marshes, but are more commonly encountered on fields and meadows further inland, where many spend the winter in Britain and Ireland.

Dotterel *Eudromias morinellus* 24 cm

A typical mountain bird, very occasionally seen on the coast during migration. Apart from the Scandinavian mountain range, the Highlands of Scotland and the Alps, isolated pairs breed on cultivated land close to the Dutch polders at sea level. Smaller than the golden plover. Adults in breeding plumage have reddish brown underparts, grey breast and back, white throat and conspicuous white 'eyebrows'.

Grey plover

Golden plover

Dotterel

juvenile

summer

juvenile

Grey plover

♂ northern

♀ southern

juvenile

Golden plover

Turnstone *Arenaria interpres* 23 cm

In summer its dappled red, black and white plumage is striking, whether at rest or on the wing. Juveniles resemble adult birds in winter plumage but have light, reddish brown feather edges. Turnstones look sturdy. Their warning cry is very distinctive, accelerating towards the end rather like the vibration of a metal ruler against a desk lid – 'te-witt-e-ewitt-e-wittededededede'. The timbre is very unusual, also distinguishable in other hoarse and nasal warning cries and in the flight call 'tuck' or 'tuck-a-tuck'. A tundra-breeding bird, on migration and in winter turnstones occur on most shores, but prefer seaweed-covered rocks.

Grey phalarope *Phalaropus fulicarius* 20.5 cm

In summer dress the male's colours, unusually, are more subdued than the female's. In all plumages it can be distinguished from the red-necked by its thicker and shorter beak and, in flight, by broader white wing bands and consistently pale grey wing coverts. Recognition is most difficult in winter dress, but by late autumn and winter, when most grey phalaropes are observed, the red-necked has already migrated. Its call is a soft, low 'drit'. Breeds mainly in Iceland and Spitsbergen and only rarely seen migrating along the coasts of western Europe. Away from the breeding grounds it is a bird of the open oceans, feeding on plankton. Winters mainly off West Africa, although those driven astray by storms may spend mild winters further north.

Red-necked phalarope *Phalaropus lobatus* 18 cm

Readily identified by its needle-thin bill and swimming habits: spins around in the water, stirring up plankton and other small creatures, devouring them at incredible speed. The male has only a dull reddish brown patch around his neck and his dress is otherwise paler. In winter, the mantle is pale ash grey with broad white stripes. The juvenile has reddish fawn fringes above, while the sides of its breast are olive green. The trim red-necked phalarope easily lifts from the water into rapid and nervous flight. Flying past, the woodpecker-like rattling notes of its call are often all one has time to notice – a short 'kirrik' or 'kitt'. It is a widespread breeding bird in northern Europe, but compared with other waders it is not much in evidence further south on migration unless storm-driven. Like the grey phalarope it is a true seabird in winter, but it also frequents the Persian Gulf and seas to the east of Africa.

Turnstone

Grey phalarope

Red-necked phalarope

juvenile

summer

Turnstone

♀ summer

winter

Grey phalarope

juvenile

♀ summer

Red-necked phalarope

Avocet *Recurvirostra avosetta* 42–46 cm

Few birds equal the avocet's grace. Differs from other waders by its brilliant black and white markings and up-curved bill. Yet, along flat coastal marshes and shallow lagoons where it breeds, it often vanishes among the throng of other birds of the seashore. Its distinctive note makes it immediately noticeable: an anxious-sounding 'plitt, plitt'. When searching for food it sways its head from side to side and uses its upward-turned beak to skim off the small creatures in the surface water. It prefers wading in about 10 cm of water, but can swim with its webbed feet. Breeding numbers have increased recently, and although most migrate south, a few estuaries harbour avocets through the winter.

Curlew *Numenius arquata* 56–63 cm

Likely to be confused with the whimbrel, but it differs in its call, head markings and longer bill (see also below). One of our commonest waders, it breeds on moors, in bogs and wet meadows. It is even more common as a winter visitor, but then occurs mostly on the coast, preferring shallow, sandy or muddy estuaries and bays. The female starts her autumn migration as early as mid-June. Often she leaves the male to rear their young by himself. The male's desolate, flute-like bubbling tones are a sign of spring, when the mood of courtship is also echoed by the soft, flute-like 'co-ee' or 'kloyit' of the birds in flight.

Whimbrel *Numenius phaeopus* 43–47 cm

The striped crown and the call, a laughing rolling trill, often of seven elements, that is nearly as melodious as the curlew's: these are its most dependable characteristics. The head markings may be difficult to spot against the light, or against glittering water, but the shorter, slightly thicker bill and faster wing beats are often useful in distinguishing this species from the curlew. Note that young curlews which are not full grown have shorter bills than the adults. In general the whimbrel looks darker than the curlew, and in flight the primaries often look very dark. Breeds on the tundra, bogs and moorland well to the north in Europe, and on some northwestern islands. During autumn and spring, however, regularly seen along the coasts, migrating to and from its wintering areas along the coasts of West Africa.

Avocet

Curlew

Whimbrel

juvenile

Avocet

Curlew

Whimbrel

Black-tailed godwit *Limosa limosa* 40–44 cm

Prefers to breed in damp meadows or marshes, often close to water. On migration and in wintering places it sometimes keeps company with the bar-tailed godwit. The different wing and tail markings of these two species (see p. 84) make them impossible to confuse when seen in flight. The black-tailed has the more elegant bearing of the two, but compared with the sturdier, shorter-legged bar-tailed godwit, black-tailed adults tend to look overgrown, and their elegance verges on lankiness. These characteristics may be difficult to assess when the birds are feeding in deep water. The black-tailed godwit in breeding dress has a white, more or less dark-blotched belly and the shade of its red is warmer and paler than in the male bar-tailed. The Icelandic (*islandica*) race, however, is usually a deeper shade of red, and some specimens have red patches all the way down the belly. The first beautiful pastel-ochre dress of the juveniles varies in its redness, but they do not have the same clearly striped mantle and back as juvenile bar-tailed godwits. In winter plumage, black-tailed are slightly greyer and more uniformly coloured. Note the difference in beak shape between the two. The notes of the black-tailed godwit are loud and shrill, and its flight call is 'vicka-vicka-vicka' or 'vi-vi-vi'. Black-tailed godwits on their breeding grounds are uneasy and very noisy, often perching like redshank on fence poles.

Bar-tailed godwit *Limosa lapponica* 33–42 cm

Common and regularly observed, not only during autumn migration but also – more than many other arctic-breeding waders – during the spring. The female's summer dress has only a slight suggestion of reddish brown, which makes her easily distinguishable from the male during spring migration. Males also vary in colour intensity and at their most magnificent are bright red underneath, with mottled brownish red on the upper parts and, in some cases, conspicuously grey wings. Juvenile plumage is similar to old birds in winter, but is more yellowish grey and the patterning of the upper parts resembles the curlew (see p. 84). Lacks the striking white wing markings of the black-tailed godwit in all plumages, and the body shape, mode of flight and overall impression may be confused with the whimbrel, but the two can be distinguished by beak shape. The female bar-tailed is slightly larger than the male and has a slightly longer upturned beak and white tail bars set close together. The flight call resembles the black-tailed godwit in tone, but it is faster and more nasal, 'view-view' or 'ved-ved-ved-ved . . .' Winters often in large flocks along the tidal beaches of western Europe.

Black-tailed godwit

Bar-tailed godwit

juvenile

summer

Black-tailed godwit

winter

♂ summer

♀ winter

Bar-tailed godwit

Common sandpiper *Tringa hypoleucos* 20 cm

Primarily a lake and river bird, but during migration found by the seashore. Conspicuous by its nervous, jerky movements, long and constantly wagging tail and predilection for stones. Prefers concealed areas of the shore with vegetation, or stones on the water's edge. Seldom spotted until startled, then rises almost from under the feet. With a succession of staccato, needle-sharp 'hee-dee-dee' calls it takes off, skimming low over the water until, almost invariably, it alights on a stone. The pale wing bars and the flight on wings alternating between vibration and gliding are unmistakable. Old birds display dark markings in summer, but in winter resemble juveniles. Temminck's stint (p. 78) is smaller; its behaviour and call are different. Common sandpipers often migrate in small flocks, which can regularly be seen at various wet localities inland.

Green sandpiper *Tringa ochropus* 23 cm

The posture and body shape are midway between the wood and common sandpiper. Like the former it is often put to flight by a human intruder, disappearing with a floppy, snipe-like wing motion. Its call when taking to the wing is a shrill, percussive, 'vit-avit' or 'twit-vit-vit' – sharper than the wood sandpiper and less clearly articulated than the common sandpiper. Its wings are broader than the wood sandpiper's and dark underneath in contrast to the topside. The upper part of the rump seems startlingly white and the dark tail bars are thicker. Mainly a lake and sewage farm bird, it occasionally appears along the sea coast and on the marshes during migration and in winter.

Wood sandpiper *Tringa glareola* 21 cm

More long-legged and graceful than the common and green sandpipers. Adults vary from grey to a distinctly brownish hue, which is less common. The upper parts of the juvenile birds are neatly speckled, varying from off-white to bright yellow. The legs are usually greenish, very rarely yellowish. In flight the wood can be distinguished from the green sandpiper by paler wings (seen from below) and by its call. The flight tone consists mainly of a pleasant whistling 'chiff-iff-iff', which becomes sharper and more temperamental when the bird is disturbed. During spring migration the breeding display call is a rapid yodelling 'liltie-liltie-liltie . . .' resembling the redshank. Occasionally seen on autumn migration by the seashore, preferring mud flats and seaweed banks, but more regularly in western Europe on swampy areas and sewage farms, often well inland.

Common sandpiper

Green sandpiper

Wood sandpiper

Common sandpiper

summer

juvenile

Green sandpiper
juvenile

juvenile

summer

Wood sandpiper

Redshank *Tringa totanus* 28 cm

The most striking features are bright red legs, red beak base and white trailing edges to the wings. The only 'sandpiper' breeding commonly on the coast (as well as on inland marshes). Often perches on fence posts. It is ahead of most other species in warning of an approaching enemy. Intruders are cautioned with a persistent hammering 'klee-klee-klee-klee' of an even intensity. The male's courtship call, alternately accelerating and diminishing yodellings, is much gentler. The flight note, 'tyu-hu, tyu-hu', can be confused with the call of the greenshank but the latter is usually tri-syllabic. In flight the wings' conspicuous white rear edges distinguish the redshank from all other waders. Juveniles lack the red at the base of the bill, and their legs are very pale red. Redshanks of all ages can appear similar to spotted redshanks, but are always distinguishable by their wing markings, shorter legs and by beak shape. In winter it is less speckled and a more uniform shade of grey.

Spotted redshank *Tringa erythropus* 32 cm

Breeds in high northern latitudes and winters in Africa and Europe, mainly around the Mediterranean but also in a few western coastal areas. During summer and autumn, and more occasionally in spring, can be seen on migration in small numbers on sandy and muddy seashores and creeks, the old birds as early as June or July, the younger ones between July and September. The immaculate, coal-black birds appear in early summer but have a motley appearance later when they start to moult. The lighter-coloured birds are often juveniles, with long orange-red legs (sometimes ochre), a feature shared only by the redshank and some adult ruffs. They have dark markings all over their underparts, whereas in juvenile redshanks these markings are only on the breast. Leg colour can be hard to see, because they prefer wading in deep water and will often actually swim. Wading, when they utilize their full length, emphasizes the gracefulness of this species and its slim body; their long narrow necks look almost serpentine as they twist and turn above and below the water's surface. The bill is also strikingly long and narrow, ending with a slight but distinct up-curve. In flight the frail, elongated body looks blunt and spindle-shaped because they habitually hold their legs forward. The rapid wing beats and straight, purposeful flight are not normally associated with *Tringas*. The upper part of the rump, particularly in summer, is a striking white, which runs well forward in a wedge up the back. The flight tone is a sharp but mellifluous whistling 'che-witt'.

Redshank

Spotted redshank

summer

Redshank

juvenile

Spotted redshank
juvenile

summer

winter

Spotted redshank

Greenshank *Tringa nebularia*   30–35 cm

The largest of the *Tringa* waders. Impressive and graceful when hunting for food. In summer, plumage has black markings on back and wings; in winter it resembles the juvenile, often with a conspicuously pale head and throat during autumn. Its flight call is a tri-syllabic whistling, 'two-two-two'. Often it is a gentle flute-like sound, but taking to the wing its call has the shrillness of a redshank. The greenshank's flight is flappier than that of the spotted redshank, and its wings, neck and legs look long and pointed. Once on the wing it often retracts its legs. Breeds in northern Europe, including Scotland, but during migration can be seen, singly or in small numbers, resting or feeding along the coast or beside coastal or inland marshy waterways or lakes. Some winter in the extreme west.

Ruff *Philomachus pugnax*   ♂ ruff 30 cm   ♀ reeve 24 cm

Both ruff (male) and reeve (female) show varied plumages during spring, but males have ruffs and ear tufts. After breeding and in winter (June–July and onwards) the male resembles the winter female but is often more greyish white and quite often has reddish orange legs for some time after moulting. In spring the female acquires a greater or lesser element of more variegated plumage and is then mottled on the breast and throat (sometimes predominantly dark in colour). Most autumn migrants are juveniles, as the old birds, especially the ruffs, migrate as early as June and July to their wintering haunts in Africa south of the Sahara. The basic colour of the young birds varies from dark brownish red to drab yellowish grey. In its typical, often erect posture the neck looks long and thick. The ruff prefers muddy beaches, lagoons or even sewage farms inland. Flight is more sluggish than other waders, and the wing beats are characteristic – slow and rather short. In flight they display a narrow wing-band, while the tail coverts form two white oval patches or a U-shaped marking. Relatively silent, but sometimes emits a meek 'too-ee' in flight.

Greenshank

Ruff

Ruff spring

summer

juvenile

Greenshank

♀ summer

♀ winter

♂ juvenile

Ruff

Temminck's stint   *Calidris temminckii*   15 cm

Adults are squatter than little stints and have more elongated bodies, although juveniles have rounder bellies. During autumn migration (in July) adults always have a few strong-grey 'winter feathers'. Lighter-coloured legs, white (not grey) outer tail feathers, a greyer impression and a differently shaped body distinguish it from the little stint. The flight note is a distinctive ringing 'tirr', often more or less continuous. When disturbed on the ground, it rises rapidly and jerkily skywards, while the little stint will often fly away close to the water's surface. An uncommon migrant in western Europe, seen most often on marshy areas near the coast or inland, but occasionally feeding along the seashore.

Little stint   *Calidris minuta*   14 cm.

More common, widespread and gregarious than Temminck's, and a characteristic ingredient of mixed *Calidris* flocks during August and September. Juveniles are more numerous than adults. The latter are distinguished from Temminck's by the white double-V on their backs, longer and black legs, and a different posture (cf. the American *Calidris* sandpipers p. 89). Perky and comical with white rounded bellies, they scamper feverishly on marshy pools and sandy shores. Magnificent in full breeding plumage which, however, loses much of its freshness and brilliance as summer wanes. Besides Temminck's stint, it resembles the sanderling to some degree but outside the breeding season the two are distinguished by the sanderling's extremely pale grey back and larger size. In winter little stints have white underparts and are grey above with darker markings. The note is not very loud and can be difficult to hear – a short, single 'pitt' or 'chick', or sometimes, mostly in breeding grounds, a repetitive 'hee-hee-hee-hee-hee-hee ...'

Sanderling   *Calidris alba*   20 cm

The broad wing bar, bright white when the bird is in the air, is a distinctive feature in all plumages. In summer dress the upper parts and breast assume varying shades of russet but some individuals remain almost black and white, like juveniles. The breast is more mottled than striped. The call is a loud descending 'plitt' or 'critt', similar to the flight note of the Kentish plover, although sometimes it resembles the 'tuck' of the turnstone. Breeding far north in the Arctic, sanderlings are regular migrants along the coasts of western Europe. They haunt extensive sandy shores but during migration they may occur on other types. Dart restlessly along the water line.

Temminck's stint   Little stint   Sanderling

juvenile

Temminck's stint

summer

uvenile

summer

Little stint

juvenile

summer

winter

Sanderling

Dunlin *Calidris alpina*   17–20 cm

The most common of the small waders, occurring in winter in flocks of from a few birds to many thousands. At least two races may be encountered: the larger, longer-billed northern race (*alpina*) and the altogether smaller southern race (*schinzii*). The southern race breeds on coastal marshes and meadows, and on low-latitude moors. In summer the dunlin has black belly markings which are less conspicuous in the southern race. Juvenile plumage varies; the sides of the belly often have dense dark patches, giving the illusion of an adult's dark belly markings. When moulting into winter plumage has begun, these patches gradually disappear, and the back and shoulders acquire a few grey winter feathers. The overall impression, then, is more yellowish grey, until in full winter dress the birds are all brownish grey except for white underparts. The dunlin is squatter than the curlew sandpiper with shorter legs and sometimes has a shorter, less curved bill. In flight it reveals a pale wing bar, white sides to the black rump and light grey outer tail feathers (see below). Sanderlings have a shorter and blunter bill and much more conspicuous wing bars. The purple sandpiper in winter is darker grey on top with yellow legs. A flock of dunlin in search of food makes a variety of almost grunting noises. The flight call is a hoarse and slightly rolling 'krrri'. The territorial male in summer has a tittering, trilling song flight high over the breeding grounds.

Curlew sandpiper *Calidris ferruginea*   18–21 cm

Summer plumage is unmistakable. Frequently associates with dunlins, but in silhouette has longer legs and bill, statelier posture, longer tail and wings and often a more rounded body. Adults seen for a short period in western and northern Europe during autumn migration have usually started their moult, and most have left or reached their African wintering places by the time it is completed. Winter plumage resembles the dunlin but is paler. Many curlew sandpipers in our area are juveniles, with 'scalier' upper parts than young dunlins and a different shape. In fresh plumage there is a dash of orange ochre on the sides of their breasts and upper parts, but rapid wear on their feathers causes this colour to fade into yellowish grey. In flight the undivided white rump forms a horseshoe. The flight call is an attractive bell-like 'krilli' (kril'l'l'li), similar to the dunlin's, although less nasal, with a timbre more like that of Temminck's stint.

Dunlin

Curlew sandpiper

winter

summer

Dunlin

juvenile

juvenile
Curlew sandpiper

summer

Curlew sandpiper

moulting summer → winter

Knot *Calidris canutus* 25 cm

A strikingly sturdy and robust wader with a distinctive size and plump stature. In its rapid and confident flight it displays surprisingly long and slender wings. Emits a short 'keut' or 'knot' in flight. The call is not very loud, but has a special nasal, somewhat gooselike quality. Breeds in the extreme Arctic, winters in large flocks along the coasts of western Europe, down as far as West Africa or even further south. Most winter around the British Isles and in the North Sea area, attracted by the extensive tidal shores. Spring passage is brief, but many birds are in the handsome breeding plumage, which is worn and moulting by the time they return.

Broad-billed sandpiper *Limicola falcinellus* 17 cm

A very rare visitor to coastal areas in western Europe. Adults resemble juveniles, but during autumn migration (July–August) they are darker, with a strikingly dark breast and often with thick dark markings along the sides of the belly. It is most reminiscent of the dunlin, with which it sometimes associates, but can be distinguished from it by the pale stripes on its back and crown. Most individuals in one area are in juvenile or summer plumage. Winter plumage resembles the dunlin's, but it has dark 'wing knuckles' like the sanderling. Its flight call is a prolonged rolling, almost buzzing 'chrryit', often combined with a shorter 'drit'.

Purple sandpiper *Calidris maritima* 23 cm

Sandpipers generally are rather squat, but the purple is the dumpiest of them all. Its legs are short (pale orange, yellow in winter) and its body is almost duck-shaped. In winter the bill is orange-yellow at the base, and slightly down-curved. Prefers the extremities of the shoreline, where the waves are broken by rocks. Similar to the little stint in the way it darts eagerly among breakers and spray. Moults while still in its breeding grounds, and by the time it reaches our coasts in autumn – often late – it is mainly clad in winter dress. Summer plumage is also very dark, with bronze-yellow and brown edges to the back feathers and dark patches close together on its underparts. The legs are greyish green. In flight, looks very dark and reveals a pale thin wing bar. The centre of its rump is dark, the edges white. Its call is a short, variable 'keutt' or 'kvitt', or sometimes, when squabbling over food, a more protracted 'kveeut'.

Knot

Broad-billed sandpiper

Purple sandpiper

winter

summer

Knot   juvenile

juvenile

Broad-billed sandpiper

winter

Purple sandpiper

Whimbrel

Curlew

Black-tailed godwit

juvenile
Bar-tailed godwit

winter

Grey plover
juvenile

Avocet

Golden plover   juvenile

Green sandpiper

Wood sandpiper

Redshank

Spotted redshank
juvenile

Greenshank

Ruff juvenile

Kentish plover

Ringed plover

Little ringed plo

Turnstone

juvenile   Red-necked phalarope

Grey phalarop
winter

Common sandpiper

Sanderling
juvenile

Dunlin
summer

Dunlin
juvenile

little stint
juvenile

Temminck's stint
juvenile

Curlew sandpiper
juvenile

Purple sandpiper
winter

Knot   juvenile

Broad-billed
sandpiper

summer

Short-billed dowitcher
juvenile

Long-billed dowitcher
juvenile

Buff-breasted
juvenile sandpiper

Lesser yellowlegs
winter

Wilson's phalarope   wint

Long-billed dowitcher (*Limnodromus scolopaceus*) 30 cm. In flight, white upper rump and lower back areas, white wing bar, relatively pale secondaries. Call a single or repeated hoarse 'kiik'. Prefers freshwater shores. **Short-billed dowitcher** (*L. griseus*) 29 cm. Similar to long-billed, but warmer beige. Emits a vocal 'tu-tu-tu'. **Buff-breasted sandpiper** (*Tryngites subruficollis*) 20 cm. No wing bars. Call a short hoarse 'tik'. Habitat: short grass. **Lesser yellowlegs** (*Tringa flavipes*). Like slender redshank, with white rump but without wing bars. Soft, monosyllabic call. **Greater yellowlegs** (*T. melanoleuca*) larger and more like greenshank, call louder. **Wilson's phalarope** (*Phalaropus tricolor*) 23 cm. More graceful than the red-necked phalarope. Lacks wing

Pectoral
sandpiper
juvenile

White-rumped
sandpiper
juvenile

ird's sandpiper
enile

Semi-palmated
sandpiper
juvenile

Least sandpiper
juvenile

bars. **Pectoral sandpiper** (*Calidris melanotos*) 18 cm. The most common transatlantic visitor, very indistinct wing bar, call a hoarse 'krrit', singly or repeatedly. **White-rumped sandpiper** (*C. fuscicollis*) 18 cm. Rump white, call a rather shrill 'yeet-yeet'. **Baird's sandpiper** (*C. bairdii*) 17 cm. Similar to white-rumped sandpiper, centre of rump dark, wing bar indistinct, call a somewhat vibrant 'kriit'. **Semi-palmated sandpiper** (*C. pusilla*) 14.5 cm. Similar to little stint, insignificantly larger, call a variable 'krit', 'chruk', lower and less pronounced than the little stint's. **Least sandpiper** (*C. minutilla*) 13 cm. Pale legs, thin bill, behaviour reminiscent of Temminck's stint. Call a light, rather protracted 'kriip'.

Skuas (*Stercorariidae*)

A group of birds which, while resembling gulls and terns, have predominantly brown plumage. Except during the breeding season, they are maritime, often living in the open oceans. They sometimes feed like gulls, but usually subsist to a great extent by robbing other birds (see Arctic skuas, p. 92).

Gulls and terns (*Laridae*)

Gulls (subfamily *Larinae*) are one of the most characteristic ingredients of seashore fauna. They could be termed the crows of the seashore, since they are omnivores, eating both living creatures (fish, the eggs and young of other birds, shellfish, crustaceans and worms) and various carrion and refuse. The juvenile plumage is mostly a mottled greyish brown. Later it is gradually replaced by the adult dress, usually grey, black and white (see p. 18 for moulting gulls). The smaller species, e.g. black-headed gull, take about a year and a half and the larger ones, e.g. herring gull, about four years to reach complete adult plumage. When identifying young gulls it is important to note these plumage changes and the great individual variations occurring in the moulting cycle. Thus the development of the common gull's first winter plumage (grey mantle) may not be completed until late winter or spring (age about 10 months), although normally it comes during September and October (age about five months). Fading and wear and tear also greatly affect the bird's appearance. The colour of the bill and legs, its shape and size, behaviour and mode of flight are other important characteristics for recognition purposes.

Terns (subfamily *Sterninae*) are more slender and swallow-like than gulls. They feed mainly on living fish and other aquatic creatures, usually obtained by diving. In addition to the species included here there are three *Childonias* species in Europe. They breed on fresh water, but during migration the black tern (*C. niger*), 24 cm, can also be seen along the coasts of northern and western Europe. During summer the black tern's head and underparts are coal black, while its upper parts are grey. In winter it is white underneath but with striking dark markings on the crown and the sides of its throat. The juvenile terns resemble the adults in winter, but their upper parts are browner. The *Chlidonias* terns are distinguished by their extremely graceful flight, often dipping down to the water, but not plunging in.

On the left opposite, top to bottom: juvenile little gull, first winter; two common gulls in first winter plumage; three-year-old great black-backed gull and three herring gulls, adult winter, three-year-old and first winter. On the right, top to bottom: adult and juvenile black-headed gull in winter; herring gull, first winter; great black-backed gull, first winter; herring gull, first winter and year-old Iceland gull (bill atypical, because it mostly looks completely dark during the first year – see picture in flight, p. 104).

Great skua   *Stercorarius skua*   52–61 cm

The great skua can be recognized by the white patches on its wings, which in flight are far more conspicuous than in other skuas. Strikingly solid in appearance, broad-winged and short in the tail, it has a sturdier appearance than young gulls. Its flight is more indolent and meandering than the gull's. The great skua breeds locally in sparsely populated colonies where it will viciously attack an intruder, sweeping down or alternatively attacking each side of the head with great accuracy. At the same time it makes short, deep 'tuck, tuck' noises. In flight its note is a deep, scolding 'ah-eish'. It robs other birds, by attacking them in flight and forcing them to drop their food, but it also eats fish, small aquatic creatures, eggs, nestlings and carrion.

Arctic skua   *Stercorarius parasiticus*
47–52 cm   including 8–10 cm tail projection

This skua has various colour phases. In addition to those shown opposite, there is a pale phase showing bars across the breast, like that of many Pomarine skuas (see p. 95). The Arctic skua is outstanding in its gracefulness, agility and harmonious proportions. Its silhouette alone distinguishes it from gulls. Often has a hawk-like flight, with rapid wing beats alternating with long glides. The tail projection of the Pomarine skua is wider and the feathers are turned at the tips to form a distinct lump at the end. Also, the Pomarine skua is larger and more heavily built, its flight more ponderous and its beak thicker. Juvenile skuas vary greatly in appearance, and it is difficult to separate the three smaller species in this plumage. During the two years approximately it takes to acquire adult dress, they stay mainly in their wintering places in tropical waters. The long-tailed skua, compared with the juvenile Arctic, is lighter grey, there is a contrast between the coverts and primaries underneath its wings, with more distinct white wing patches. At close quarters one may possibly distinguish longer central tail feathers while there is hardly any visible projection in juvenile Arctics. The Arctic skua breeds near the sea on grassy bogs, often at high altitudes, in remote mainland areas and offshore islands in northern Europe. It lives mainly by stealing food from gulls, terns and other birds, chasing and diving at its victim to drop or disgorge the prey. It also takes eggs, nestlings, small rodents, fish and other aquatic creatures.

Great skua

Arctic skua

Great skua

light phase

Arctic skua

dark phase

Great skua

juvenile

juvenile

Long-tailed skua

Long-tailed skua *Stercorarius longicaudus*

51–60 cm   including 13–25 cm tail projection

Breeds in high mountain country and tundra throughout the northern hemisphere, but a very rare coastal migrant in western Europe. Distinguished by its slender silhouette, graceful flight and very long tail projection (see also Arctic skua, p. 92). Wintering areas as for Pomarine skua.

94–95

Pomarine skua *Stercorarius pomarina*

48–51 cm   including 5–7 cm tail projection

For recognition features see Arctic skua (p. 92).
Breeds mostly on coast of Arctic Ocean, from
the White Sea and further east. Observed on
European coasts during migration to and from
its wintering places in the seas off West Africa.

Pomarine skua

juvenile

Arctic skua

juvenile

Arctic skua

dark phase

Common gull *Larus canus* 41–45 cm

The softer head shape, dark eye, thinner beak and smaller size distinguishes it from the herring gull. White patches at the wing tips distinguish it from the kittiwake. The juvenile has a mottled brown mantle, replaced during autumn (seldom later) by steel grey, its first winter dress. Dark patches on the underparts, head and throat, however, like the contrast on the tops of the wings, are extremely variable, but gradually become paler towards the first summer. Distinguished from the Mediterranean gull by a thinner, less down-curved beak, darker mantle, less conspicuous facial mask (sometimes lacking altogether) and longer and narrower wings. Second winter plumage resembles the adult's, but the primary coverts are dark and patches on the tips of the wings are smaller. The call has a characteristic tone, a variable 'kiew', 'ah', 'caowee' or 'keh-khe-khe-khe . . .' Breeds on various types of seashore, on lakesides or beside large rivers, living on fish, molluscs and crustaceans as well as insects and worms from forays in fields and meadows.

Kittiwake *Rissa tridactyla* 42–46 cm

In adult dress is readily distinguished from the common gull by the Indian-ink black of its wing tips and almost always dark legs. Young birds up to about a year have black zigzag wing markings. The little gull in its first winter dress is considerably smaller, has a more wavering, butterfly-like flight, slight shading on its crown and grey markings on its secondaries. Essentially a maritime bird, the kittiwake often follows ships far out to sea. It breeds in large colonies on precipitous cliffs, and sometimes on window-ledges of buildings or other artificial 'crags'. It is very noisy on its breeding grounds, bawling with a shrill and somewhat nasal 'kiew-aarrk' and a hoarse 'kek-kek-kek-kek'. Lives mainly on small marine creatures, fish and fish guttings.

Black-headed gull *Larus ridibundus* 38–44 cm

Easily recognized by distinctive markings on both sides of its wings and, in summer dress, by a velvet brown crown. In juvenile plumage the upper parts and crown are a warm reddish brown. In first winter dress (p. 102) it may be confused with the Mediterranean gull, but the head, wing markings and shape of the bill distinguishes it. The young retain diagonal wing markings until their first summer. The call is unusual, something like 'weiaouv' or 'aurkk'. A very common bird seen near most coastal centres and inland waters, and often in town centres or fields. It lives on all kinds of invertebrate animals, and sometimes refuse.

Common gull   Kittiwake   Black-headed gull

Common gull

winter

Kittiwake

winter

Black-headed gull

summer

Herring gull *Larus argentatus* 58–67 cm

The young bird's variable plumage makes it easy to confuse with other gulls. Year-old and two-year-old herring gulls with faded wing feathers may be confused with the glaucous or Iceland gulls, but they always show some pigmentation in their primaries. Herring–glaucous hybrids can occur. The herring gull has different beak markings from subadult glaucous gulls and thicker dark markings. In second winter plumage it may be confused with first winter common gulls, but the smaller size of the latter, the more regular tail bars and slimmer beaks distinguishes them. The herring gull's call is 'aou', sometimes round and short, sometimes long and shrill, often in long succession. Its warning cry is a deep scolding 'ag-ag-ag-ag . . .'. The squeaky penetrating call of young birds becomes harsher as they mature until the voice finally 'breaks'. The herring gull frequents seashores, large lakes, towns and rubbish dumps. Its varied diet consists of living and dead animals washed up on the shore, eggs, nestlings and refuse. Nests in loose colonies, usually on rocky islands or cliffs, but increasingly inland, sometimes on tall buildings.

Glaucous gull *Larus hyperboreus* 64–81 cm

Markedly larger than the herring gull, its build is similar to the great black-backed gull. Pale primaries, white in adult dress, distinguish it from the herring gull. The best way to tell it from the Iceland gull is by its stouter bill, more angular head shape and relatively shorter wings, although in all gull species the female is smaller and more slender than the male. Until it is about two years old it has a differently coloured beak from the herring and first winter Iceland gulls – between pale flesh colour and greyish white, with the outer third dark and clearly demarcated. Its habits and habitats resemble those of the herring gull but its call is lower pitched. Scarce in Britain.

Iceland gull *Larus glaucoides* 56–64 cm

Usually of slighter build than the glaucous gull, it has a shorter bill, more rounded head profile, shorter legs, slimmer and longer wings and faster wing beats. A juvenile has a dark grey, black-tipped beak which looks completely dark from a distance. During the second winter and after, however, its bill resembles the glaucous gull's in colour. As a one-year-old (second winter) it has almost completely white plumage with isolated brown feathers. Habitat, behaviour and call are similar to the herring gull. Scarce in Britain.

Herring gull

Glaucous gull

Iceland gull

juvenile

Herring gull

Glaucous gull
winter

winter

Iceland gull

Great black-backed gulls

Great black-backed gull   *Larus marinus*   64–79 cm

Adult birds might be confused with Scandinavian lesser black-backed gulls, but the latter have yellow legs and in flight display less white at the wing tips. Females, seen in the field, are distinctly smaller and slimmer, with a thinner bill than males. This species normally acquires its first leaden grey mantle feathers during its second year. In its first winter there is more plumage contrast than on the herring gull (lighter base colour and heavier dark markings), but there is *less* contrast between its primaries and secondaries. The beak is completely dark during the first year and more variable during the second. The head and beak are more angular and massive than other gulls. Its habits resemble those of other gulls, but it is not as numerous. Many winter well out to sea, but juveniles may scavenge inland. During the breeding season it lives on eggs and nestlings of other seabirds. The call is a heavier, more 'double-bass' sound than that of the lesser black-backed gull.

Lesser black-backed gull   *Larus fuscus*   53–59 cm

The adult plumage colour of the western European race (*graellsii*) is somewhat like that of the dark herring gull, but the Scandinavian race is so dark that it is similar only to the greater black-backed gull. Legs of the lesser black-backed gull, however, vary between whitish yellow and bold orange-yellow, not pink. Juveniles differ from juvenile herring gulls in the relatively slight contrast between primaries and secondaries, broader bars on the tail and give a darker overall impression. Back and shoulders take on a dull grey base colour in the first winter (cf. herring gull and great black-backed gull) and then gradually darken. Habitat, call and diet are similar to the herring gull. Lesser black-backed gulls may nest in large colonies, usually on vegetated slopes on coast or islands, but occasionally inland. Mainly migrant in western Europe.

Great black-backed gull

Lesser black-backed gull

Great black-backed gull

Scandinavian

western

Lesser black-backed gull

Mediterranean gull (*Larus melano-cephalus*) 39 cm. Breeds in southeast Europe. Winters in coastal areas up to the channel. Adult white and grey, no dark wing markings and black head in summer.

Common gull
first winter

Mediterranean gull
first winter

Black-headed gull
first winter

Kittiwake
juvenile
autumn–winter

Ivory gull
first winter

Sabine's gull
juvenile   autumn

Little gull
first winter

adult   winter

Ivory gull (*Pagophila eburnea*) 44 cm. Extreme Arctic, almost never outside the ice floe belt of the Arctic Ocean. Graceful tern-like flight. Adults are pure white. Avoids sitting on the water.

Sabine's gull (*Larus sabini*) 33 cm. Breeds in North America and Greenland. Winters at sea. Rarely observed off the coasts of western Europe, then mainly between August and November. An effortless, graceful, tern-like flight, indented tail and striking tri-angular wing markings distinguish it from other gulls. Adults are uniformly grey but juveniles are brownish grey, with a grey cap in summer.

Little gull (*Larus minutus*) 28–30 cm. Breeds in northeast Europe, locally in Scandinavia. Regularly seen during migration, sometimes inland, and while wintering by the sea. Adult wings have unmistakable dark undersides but juveniles (summer–autumn) have a brown-black mantle, neck and crown. Flight rather flappy.

Herring gull   first winter

Herring gull   second winter

Iceland gull   first winter

Glaucous gull   first winter

Lesser black-backed gull
juvenile

Great black-backed gull
juvenile

Great black-backed gull
second winter

western

Common gull

Herring gull

Lesser black-backed gull

juvenile

winter

Gull-billed tern

Sandwich tern

juvenile

Gull-billed tern   *Gelochelidon nilotica*   39 cm

Differs in habits from other terns. On the breeding grounds it mostly hunts for food over dry land. Often catches insects over shallow water, but will not dive after fish like the Sandwich tern. During migration, when this behavioural difference is less recognizable it is easily confused with the Sandwich tern. The heavier, gull-like bill is the best distinguishing characteristic. Also it has a less sharply forked tail than the Sandwich tern, of pale grey instead of white. These differences are hard to spot. When standing it has long gull-like legs. Its call is deeper and less grating than the Sandwich tern's, a croaking 'kve(ck)-kveh-kveh-kveh' or 'cho-buk'. It lives on small insects, worms and lizards. Winters in Africa. Scarce in Britain on migration.

Sandwich tern   *Sterna sandvicensis*   41 cm

Often spotted because of its distinctive note, a less delicate 'ki-ki-ki-ki' rattle than the common tern's, a somewhat sharp 'kay-reck', or often no more than a short 'kirrick'. Young birds in autumn have a gentler call. Discovery of this bird takes time. It is a large, slender, slim-winged tern usually flying at a fair height with deep wing beats. Distinctive features are the pale, almost perfectly white dress, long, black, bristling crest and black beak with yellow tip. Often visible from a distance, it frequently hovers high over the water, plummeting for fish. Seated, it is distinguished by its crest, rather tufted at the back, and by legs which are shorter than the gull-billed tern's. The juveniles have smudgy black markings over the mantle, wing coverts and tail. A coastal bird, it lives mainly on fish and breeds in widespread colonies on islands or secluded mainland areas. At the end of the nesting season (July) most congregate in European waters with an abundance of fish. Migrates later for the winter to the coastal areas of West Africa.

Gull-billed tern

Sandwich tern

Gull-billed tern

Sandwich tern

Little tern   *Sterna albifrons*   23 cm

Like the Caspian tern, easily recognizable by its size. Both standing and in flight it has a rather shrunken look. Wing movements are much faster and jerkier than those of other terns. Juvenile plumage is similar to other terns, but with no red on legs or bill. For such a small bird it produces a loud call and is generally very noisy. The call is reminiscent of the Sandwich tern, usually a short wailing 'ee-ich' and a slightly louder, plover-like rolling 'kyrrik-ik, kyrri-ik, kyrri-ik ...' It lives on fish and small marine invertebrates. Nests in small colonies on sand or shingle beaches, where eggs and young merge remarkably well with their surroundings. Widespread.

Caspian tern   *Hydroprogne tschegrava*   48–57 cm

Easy to spot by its size, formidable bright red bill (carrot red in young birds) and dark primaries underneath. In winter the dark cap becomes mottled on the ear-coverts, forehead and crown. Juveniles have a mottled brown crown, dark patches on the mantle and indistinct dark markings on the tips of their wing feathers, wing coverts and tail coverts. Their wings are more blunt than those of adults, making a gull-like impression in flight. The note is unmistakable, and it often heralds its arrival with a very loud, grating 'kaar-uush'. The Caspian tern prefers feeding in fresh or brackish water. From its breeding grounds on secluded islands and peninsulas in the Baltic it often makes for the nearest freshwater lake or brackish creek in search of fish, its main diet. Very rarely seen in Britain, en route to wintering grounds off Africa.

Little tern

Caspian tern

Little tern

juvenile

Caspian tern

Common tern *Sterna hirundo* 36–42 cm

Distinguished from the Arctic tern in summer dress by brighter yellowish red colour, the black tip of its beak, longer legs, white underparts and darker outer primaries, which usually contrast slightly with the inner ones. Only the inner primaries are translucent. In winter plumage it has a white forehead and an almost completely black beak. Distinctive juvenile features are the black leading edge of the wing, stouter bill with a reddish base and a cinnamon-coloured mantle. The juvenile also has grey secondaries with a white outer edge forming a bar along the rear of its wing. A very noisy bird, in flight it emits a short 'kik', occasionally punctuated with a prolonged rattling 'keee-yaaah'. In breeding colonies it communicates or warns with a variety of rattling noises. Calls are more brittle than those of the Arctic tern, and slightly less grating, but in practice it is very difficult to hear the difference. The common tern is widespread and numerous, and occurs on most types of shoreline, breeding on the coast and inland. It lives on fish and shrimps.

Arctic tern *Sterna paradisaea* 36–42 cm

For field separation from the common tern, see above. Habitat, behaviour and diet are similar to those of the common tern. Sometimes the two species nest side by side. In the southern part of its area, however, the Arctic tern is more attached to the sea than its relative. It winters in southern hemisphere seas, sometimes the Antarctic Ocean, migrating an enormous distance each year.

Roseate tern *Sterna dougallii* 36–42 cm

In adult plumage it is far paler than the Arctic and common terns. With its almost completely dark bill – the base is a greater or lesser degree of red during the breeding season – it somewhat resembles a slender Sandwich tern. It has long legs and, in breeding dress, pinkish underparts. In flight it looks even more slender and graceful than other terns, mainly because of its long tail streamers, but its wings are relatively short. Juveniles have black beaks and legs, almost completely dark crowns and conspicuous black scaly markings on the mantle. In flight, roseate terns display a white trailing edge along the length of the wings and white secondaries, but unlike the common and Arctic terns, no dark outer edge on the primaries. Characteristic calls include a rapid non-rattling 'ku-yeev' and a grating 'aach'. Exclusively a marine bird, living mostly on fish, it breeds colonially on islands or secluded sandy mainland beaches mostly in Britain and Ireland. Uncommon.

Common tern

Arctic tern

Roseate tern

Common tern

Arctic tern

juvenile

Common tern

juvenile

Arctic tern

Roseate tern

Guillemot *Uria aalge*

42 cm

Upper parts shading between races. Northern guillemots (*aalge*) are as black as the razorbill. Southern races from the Baltic, southern parts of the British Isles and further south (*albionis*) are sootier with dull chocolate-brown heads. In winter, the white cheek distinguishes the guillemot from the razorbill and Brünnich's guillemot. It is also distinguished from the latter by its narrower beak and the striped sides of its belly, although this feature is less apparent in young birds. One common plumage variety (*'ringvia'*) has a narrow white eye-ring and a narrow white line (bridle) running backwards from the eye. Guillemots nest in dense colonies on accessible open sea cliff ledges and stacks, and are a principal component of the north Atlantic seabird colonies. Their calls are based on a loud grating 'arrrr' or 'oarrrr', varying in duration and combination. The young jump from nesting ledges before they can fly, and are not fully grown until late summer. Guillemots live on fish and small marine creatures.

Brünnich's guillemot *Uria lomvia*

42 cm

Completely black upper parts. The light stripe along the beak is the best distinguishing feature. In the water, however, the bill, stouter than a guillemot's, and absence of stripes on the sides of the belly give a good chance of identification at a reasonable range. In winter the dark well below the eye is distinctive but young 'black-cheeked razorbills' can have bills almost as slim as those of Brünnich's guillemots. Habit and diet similar to guillemots. Very rare off western Europe.

Razorbill *Alca torda*

41 cm

Adult unmistakable. Juveniles have a narrower beak without white markings and could be confused with Brünnich's guillemot. In the water, immature birds can be mistaken for little auks. Because razorbills are much blacker they can be distinguished from guillemots at a considerable distance. In the water razorbills are immaculate and majestic, with black upper parts, white wing bands, thick neck and blunt beak. The long tail and the white bar on the wing along the rear edge of the secondaries are conspicuous and good flight characters. Habits and diet resemble the guillemot's but colonies are smaller and scattered, and the nests often hidden in crevices on the cliff.

Guillemot

Brünnich's guillemot

Razorbill

winter

Guillemot

winter

Brünnich's guillemot

winter

Razorbill

Black guillemot   *Cepphus grylle*   33–37 cm

Unmistakable in summer, but in winter, and especially in flight, could be confused
with a small grebe. Easily recognized, however, by its straight trajectory, rapid,
whistling wing beats and conspicuous white wing patches. Young birds resemble the
adults in winter dress but are somewhat browner. Black guillemots occur in much
smaller groups than other auks but are widespread. In the breeding grounds it
produces almost improbably and irritatingly loud whistling noises, 'piñih'. From
their nests in caves and under boulders, the nesting birds, and later the young, emit
whistling calls which are not easily pinpointed. Black guillemots nest on rocky coasts
and stay nearby in winter, living on fish caught by diving close to the sea bed.

Puffin   *Fratercula arctica*   27–42 cm

Unmistakable in summer. After the breeding season loses parts of its grotesque
beak, which then becomes narrower and predominantly yellowish. Its face turns
dark grey in winter. Young birds have even thinner bills and could be confused in
flight with the little auk. The typically auk-like flight is a straight trajectory with
rapid wing movements, but on the nesting grounds they are better fliers than the
guillemot and razorbill. They glide over the nesting places with stiff wings, adjusting
their approach with whirring wings to touch down at the exact point intended, and
scamper to the nest. They excavate nests in burrows on grassy slopes and screes, often
in very large colonies, always in undisturbed places. Their diet, mostly small fish, is
caught often at some distance from the colony. Most winter in mid-ocean.

Little auk   *Plotus alle*   23–25 cm

Despite its smallness, could be confused with the young of other auks. On water the
thickset neck and head, with almost infinitesimal beak, are striking features. Distinctive flight characteristics are the oddly cigar-shaped, 'beakless' profile and whirring
wings. The undersides of the wings, if one has time to see them, are black, unlike
those of other auks. Young birds resemble the summer adults but are browner and
duller. It is scarce in the south and west and is mainly a winter visitor, from its nesting
places on rocky island coasts from Greenland in the west to Severnaya Zemlya in
Siberia to the east. Lives on molluscs, crustaceans and plankton.

Black guillemot

Puffin

Little auk

winter

Black guillemot

Puffin

juvenile

winter

Little auk

Rock dove

Rock dove   *Columba livia*

33 cm

The pigeons so common in our towns and cities are descended from the rock dove. In western Europe the rock dove occurs on sea cliffs and in nearby fields, while in other areas it mainly inhabits rocky mountain and desert terrain. It is distinguished from the stock dove and wood pigeon by black bars on its wings and a white rump. In some places escaped or feral pigeons also occur by the sea, and may be indistinguishable from rock doves. These 'tame' pigeons sometimes associate with rock doves, and crossbreeding occurs. The display flight, gliding with wings raised, and the call, a soft cooing, are identical with the feral pigeon. The rock dove lives on various seeds and plant material which it plucks from the ground.

Passerines of the seashore

Most passerine birds can be seen at some time or other by the sea, but only a few have appreciable links with the seashore in that they are largely dependent on insects or plants which in turn depend on seawater. Many passerines, whether or not they are directly linked with the seashore, often congregate on island peninsulas and promontories during migration to rest and feed before tackling the open sea, the barrier to onward migration. During the autumn one can often make anomalous discoveries such as spotted flycatchers and willow warblers eagerly hunting mosquitoes, midges and flies on banks of seaweed. But there are other species such as pied and white wagtails and starlings, which regularly hunt seaweed maggots and shrimps by the seashore. Many crows specialize in living off coastal seabird colonies with abundant supplies of eggs and nestlings as well as molluscs, crustaceans and washed-up animal corpses of all sizes. They often nest in copses close to the beach. Similarly, some lakeside birds such as reed buntings and bearded reedlings will sometimes nest in reeds near river estuaries or around freshwater lakes adjoining the seashore. In winter several tundra species make their way to the coasts of western Europe, which often have a milder climate than places further inland. Many migrating or (in winter) nomadic seed-eaters will often follow the navigation line made by the coasts. The flora of the coastal marshes, including, for instance, glasswort, annual sea-blite, grass-leaved orache and thrift, provide seed for the skylark, shore lark, twite, Lapland bunting and snow bunting, among others; plants like mugwort and spear thistle, which often grow abundantly on shingle banks, provide food for such species as the goldfinch, tree sparrow and reed bunting. The rock pipit and the chough (p. 118) are the only passerines breeding exclusively near the seashore in western and northern Europe. The shore lark, twite and snow bunting (p. 120) are included here because, unlike the skylark, starling and goldfinch, for example, they winter mainly by the sea.

Rock pipit *Anthus spinoletta* 16.5 cm

There are three main races of rock pipit in Europe. Those around the Baltic (*littoralis*) are somewhat lighter and browner in colour than the western European race (*petrosus*). *Spinoletta*, the third race (possibly a species in its own right), known as the 'water pipit', has a plain light-coloured breast in summer. The rock pipit breeds by rocky coasts and winters by seashores. It is sometimes seen with meadow pipits on coastal marshes and on seaweed banks, but is distinguished by its generally darker appearance, greater size and dark legs (other pipits have light-coloured legs). In autumn it is dull greyish green with densely marked underparts. In winter dress the water pipit is far paler than the rock pipit and its upper parts are a more uniform shabby greyish brown. The rock pipit has distinct calls, a single 'ssit' and a softer 'huit'. The water pipit, and possibly the rock pipit, has a short, rolling 'drrrt' which gives it away among groups of meadow pipits. The water pipit has white outer tail feathers while the rock pipit's are grey. A straightforward combination of bright sharp trills and scales is delivered during song flight, when the bird rises with wings flapping and then, with stiff wings, parachutes down to its take-off spot. It lives on insects, small littoral crustaceans and molluscs.

Chough *Pyrrhocorax pyrrhocorax* 40 cm

Found mostly in high mountain areas in the Mediterranean countries and the Alps, but in western Europe is associated with wild rocky coastlines. Its red bill (orange-yellow in young birds) distinguishes it from other crow species. In the Alps, however, and in mountain areas of the Mediterranean, it has a sister species, the Alpine chough (*P. graculus*), which is also completely black but with a bright yellow bill only half as long. A real acrobat, it is a playful bird. Its wings look very flexible, and in direct flight they are regularly loosely drawn in next to the body, creating an undulating flight path. The broad wings and splayed-out primaries are also striking characteristics. The call is a clear 'keee-ow' and whistling 'chee-aw', 'keee-ow' or gull-like 'kuauk-kau-kau'. Although gregarious, it is rarely seen in large flocks in western Europe. Its diet includes insects (especially ants) and their larvae, lizards, snails, fruits and berries.

Rock pipit

Water pipit

Chough

Water pipit
winter

Rock pipit   western

juvenile

Chough

Shore lark   *Eremophila alpestris*   16.5 cm

Nests on bare mountain heaths and tundra. Winters mainly along sea coasts on grassy marshes, fine shingle beaches or on fields close by. Often keeps company with skylarks, from which it is most easily distinguished by its call, although its paler and drabber sandy grey upper parts are often a striking feature in flight. It will emit a tri- or bisyllabic 'tsee-tol-tsee' or 'tse-tseeo', high pitched and sharp, with the timbre of the dunnock and a bright whistling 'tsiu' or 'piu' similar to the snow bunting. Its flight undulates more than that of the skylark, but on the ground it huddles and moves with mouse-like jerky movements. In summer the characteristic face markings are brighter yellow and black, and the male has two small 'horns' on his crown. During winter it lives on seeds.

Twite   *Acanthis flavirostris*   13.5 cm

Breeds in uplands and extreme western coastal areas but winters on coastal marshes and stubble fields. Distinguished from the linnet (*Acanthis cannabina*) by the deep curry-yellow throat, honey-coloured bill (the linnet's is dark grey) and the male's rump, which is pink. However, it lacks the red cap and black bib of the redpoll (*Acanthis flammea*), another linnet-like species. Its flight call resembles the linnet's, a hard reverberating 'chut-chululutt', but it also has a distinctive hoarse 'chiut' or 'chway'. Often occurs in flocks, living on seeds in winter.

Snow bunting   *Plectrophenax nivalis*   16.5 cm

Breeds on mountain heaths and Arctic tundra but often found on western European coasts in winter. During autumn and winter the plumage is a variable patchwork of black, white and shades of brownish grey and red ochre. In summer the male is largely white, with some black markings; young birds in autumn sometimes have only a suggestion of white. The snow bunting is distinguished from all other buntings by its mainly white wings with black tips. It often travels in fairly large flocks. The main call is a ringing 'pirrirritt', with a distinctive flute-like 'peev' or 'piew', persistently uttered by single birds or those separated from the flock. Winters on coastal marshes, sand or shingle beaches, and occasionally in open country further inland.

Shore lark

Twite

Snow bunting

Shore lark winter

Twite winter

♂

♀

Snow bunting winter

Ornithological and Conservation Societies in Britain and Ireland

Most counties and some major towns and cities have their own ornithological society: your library should be able to provide the address. Usually these societies hold regular indoor and field meetings – an ideal introduction to the area and the subject – and publish regular reports.

National bodies:

British Trust for Ornithology, Beech Grove, Tring, Herts.
(organizes bird ringing, censuses and a wide variety of studies designed for cooperative participation by amateurs, *Bird Study* quarterly, *BTO News* every two months.)

Irish Wildbird Conservancy, Royal Irish Academy, 19 Dawson Street, Dublin 2.
(fulfils a similar role in Ireland to the B.T.O.)
Royal Society for the Protection of Birds, The Lodge, Sandy, Beds.
(reserve network available to members, junior branch Young Ornithologist's Club organizes cooperative fieldwork. Colour magazine *Birds* quarterly.)

Wildfowl Trust, Slimbridge, Gloucestershire.
(network of wildfowl reserves and collections available, organizes winter wildfowl counts. Regular bulletin *Wildfowl News*, and *Wildfowl*, published annually.)

Further Reading

The following selection of books is suggested for you to follow up your interest in birds and their lives. Some deal with identification, some with fieldwork and equipment, and some with biology and ecology. All will prove useful sources of further titles.

Batten, L., Flegg, J., Sorenson, J., Wareing, M., Watson, D. and Wright, D., *Birdwatchers' Year*, T. & A. D. Poyser, 1973.

Bruun, B. and Singer, A., *The Hamlyn Guide to the Birds of Britain and Europe*, Hamlyn, 1974.

Campbell, B. and Ferguson-Lees, J., *A Field Guide to Birds' Nests*, Constable, 1972.

Cramp, S., Bourne, W. R. P. and Saunders, D., *The Seabirds of Britain and Ireland*, Collins, 1974.

Durman, R., (ed.), *Bird Observatories in Britain and Ireland*, T. & A. D. Poyser, 1976.

Fisher, J., *The Fulmar*, Collins, 1954.

Fisher, J. and Flegg, J., *Watching Birds*, T. & A. D. Poyser, 1974; Penguin Books, 1978 (in paperback).

Fisher, J. and Lockley, R. M., *Seabirds*, Collins, 1954.

Flegg, J., *Discovering Bird Watching*, Shire Publications, 1973.

Flegg, J. J. M., *Binoculars, Cameras and Telescopes*, B.T.O. Field Guide, 1971.

Fry, C. H. and Flegg, J. J. M., *World Atlas of Birds*, Mitchell Beazley, 1974.

Gooders, J., *Where to Watch Birds*, Deutsch, 1967; Pan Books, 1977 (in paperback).

Gooders, J., *Where to Watch Birds in Europe*, Deutsch, 1970; Pan Books, 1977 (in paperback).

Heinzel, H., Fitter, R. and Parslow, J., *The Birds of Britain and Europe*, Collins, 1972.

Hollom, P. A. D., *The Popular Handbook of British Birds*, H. F. & G. Witherby, 1971.

Hollom, P. A. D., *The Popular Handbook of Rarer British Birds*, H. F. & G. Witherby, 1970.

Lack, D., *Ecological Adaptations for Breeding in Birds*, Methuen, 1968.

Lack, D., *Population Studies of Birds*, Oxford University Press, 1966.

Lockley, R. M., *Shearwaters*, Dent, 1942.

Lockley, R. M., *Puffins*, Dent, 1953.

Mead, C. J., *Bird Ringing*, B.T.O. Field Guide, 1974.

Moreau, R. E., *The Palearctic-African Bird Migration System*, Academic Press, 1972.

Nethersole-Thompson, D., *The Greenshank*, Collins, 1951.

Ogilvie, M. A., *Ducks of Britain and Europe*, T. & A. D. Poyser, 1975.

Sharrock, J. T. R., (ed.), *The Atlas of Breeding Birds in Britain and Ireland*, B.T.O., 1977.

Thomson, A. L., *A New Dictionary of Birds*, Nelson, 1964.

Tinbergen, N., *The Herring Gull's World*, Collins, 1953.

Voous, K. H., *Atlas of European Birds*, Nelson, 1960.

Welty, J. C., *The Life of Birds*, Saunders, 1975.

Witherby, H. F., Jourdain, F. C. R., Ticehurst, N. F. and Tucker, B. W., *The Handbook of British Birds*, 5 vols, H. F. & G. Witherby, 1938–41.

Index